CW01655124

MEMOIRS OF A STATION MASTER

# MEMOIRS OF A STATION MASTER

(1879)

BY

ERNEST J. SIMMONS

EDITED BY

JACK SIMMONS

ADAMS & DART

Introduction and Notes © 1974 Jack Simmons
This edition first published in 1974 by Adams & Dart
1a Queen Square, Bath, Somerset
SBN 239 00124 9
Distributed by Jupiter Books Ltd
167 Hermitage Road, Harringay, London N.4
Text set in 11/12 pt. Monotype Modern, printed by letterpress,
and bound in Great Britain at The Pitman Press, Bath

# INTRODUCTION

Not many good books were written from the inside about the railway service in Victorian England. Of the few there are, nearly all are the work of senior officers, like the two that emerged from the London & North Western Company, Sir George Findlay's *Working and Management of an English Railway* and G. P. Neele's *Railway Reminiscences.* The book reprinted here is very different from those grave works. It is irreverent, sometimes passionate; perhaps not always truthful; a highly personal, indeed intimate, account of the career of a mid-Victorian stationmaster on the Great Western.

It was published anonymously at Reading in 1879, under the title *Ernest Struggles;* a second part followed in 1880. The book is rare: the British Museum does not possess a copy of this first volume, though it has one of the second.

The author, Hubert A. Simmons, was born at Twyford in Berkshire in 1839. His father, he tells us (p. 114), farmed 500 acres in the parish. He 'had been churchwarden, overseer, and had moved in good society'; but he became bankrupt, and his son Hubert, having served for a time as a farm bailiff, determined to seek his fortune in London. The book opens with a brief, a too brief, account of his work as a rent-collector in Kilburn, from which he moved at the age of twenty-one into the service of the Great Western Company. This was at the beginning of 1861. The chronology of his narrative is unfortunately clouded, and nothing will make it quite consistent. From the Company's records his service, during the period covered by this volume, appears as follows:[1]

| | | |
|---|---|---|
| Clerk | Wallingford Road | February 1861 |
| Clerk | Didcot | July 1861 |
| Station Clerk (i.e. Stationmaster) | Aynho | May 1863 |
| ,, | Thame | May 1864 |
| ,, | Twyford | September 1865 |
| ,, | Bilston | March 1866 |
| ,, | Windsor | November 1867 |

[1] British Transport Historical Records GW 15/3, 195. Despite his constant complaints about the Company's niggardliness, his salary in these posts did in fact rise steadily, from £60 to £140 a year.

The special interest of Simmons's book arises from his account of the railway service. In the jargon of our own time, he offers us a worm's-eye view. When stimulated by grievances like his, railwaymen occasionally became vocal, and so did others, on their behalf.[1] But they seldom showed anything of his humour, and very few indeed were articulate, able to make us laugh as he can when he depicts an angry Director 'going about like a captured wasp in a wine-glass' (p. 134) or characterizes a senior officer he detests as 'a groggy prevaricator' (p. 137).

How seriously can we take what he has to say? On matters of fact he is unreliable. He was writing a good time after the events he describes, and, as it seems plain, from memory. He gives us, for instance, a highly-coloured account of a 'most awful smash' at Bilston (pp. 133–34). No accident of the kind is to be found among those reported on by the Board of Trade.[2] Confronted with this discrepancy, we are naturally less disposed to credit Simmons's description of the scene in the Boardroom at Paddington that follows.

It is more difficult still to accept his estimate of persons. His portraits of the senior officers of the Great Western Company, of Gooch, and even more of Grierson and Spagnoletti, are caricatures. He is grossly unjust to the Inspectors of Railways (pp. 77–78), conscientious and hard-working civil servants to whom the travelling public and the general body of railwaymen owed a great deal. But, that said, there is much to be learnt from his attitude towards these men, and from the tone in which he criticizes them. It would be absurd to look to him for justice. The value of what he has to say lies in his point of view. The members of the Board of a railway company *were* the uncontrolled arbiters of the destiny of the men they employed. As he puts it, in a good sentence: 'Everything a railway man has of value he takes with him on the day he has to appear before his Directors' (p. 154). He speaks for thousands of his fellow railway servants when he attacks individual Directors and senior officers for stupidity, prejudice, and arrogance. They may not have been, in fact, stupid or prejudiced or arrogant; but that, we can feel tolerably sure, was how they often looked.

Simmons gives us the sense of what the ordinary railwayman of his standing felt. The standing is important. For the railway service was a

---

[1] A classic early example, at some points similar in tone to this book, is *Railway Locomotive Management*, by 'Veritas Vincit' (1847). In the mid-Victorian age, see for example the articles in *Reynold's Newspaper* in 1886, on which Karl Marx drew (*Capital*, Everyman ed., i. 255–56).

[2] There had been one at Priestfield, the next station, in 1864 (*Parl. Papers*, 1865, xlix. 126–27).

hierarchy: not only because it was part of a hierarchical society and reflected that, but also from necessity. If a complicated organization like a railway, served by machines that were always potentially dangerous, was to be made to work in order and safety, there had to be a chain of command. Every Victorian railwayman knew his place in that chain. If, like Simmons, he was somewhere near the middle of it, he was apt to be particularly conscious of his dignity. Simmons gives us no sense that he was overbearing towards those under him. But he was acutely touchy with his superiors, always jealous of his personal position and affronted by the least slight, real or supposed, that was put upon it. No doubt he was rendered more sensitive by his own social origins. The natural expectations he was born to were those of a prosperous farmer, not of a mere salaried servant to a commercial company. He was a man of some education, able to translate Ovid and to speak French after a fashion (pp. 2 and 3); in that respect at least the equal of Daniel Gooch, who, Chairman of the Great Western Company though he might become, was the son of a small Northumberland iron merchant. All this can be detected in Simmons's narrative, and it must be given its due weight in assessing the value of what he has to say.

We cannot take the dialogue in his book literally, as if he had set himself to write down every sentence he heard at the time; and it may well be that, for the reason just given, he has sharpened and roughened the tone of what he reports the Directors and officers of the Company as saying. But much of it carries the stamp of truth and is both consistent and credible.

Under the shadow of the law of libel, he unfortunately felt compelled to disguise the names of people and places under pseudonyms. The interpretation of some of them is simple: 'Hinoe' for Aynho, 'Fame' for Thame, and so on. 'Gabriel Gouge' is an obvious disguise for Daniel Gooch, 'Sprigalilly' a charming version of the name of Spagnoletti, the Signal Engineer. But many of the others present difficulties, not all of which have been solved in the present edition.[1] By the use he makes of this expedient Simmons does himself an injustice. He appears, inevitably, to be writing a work of fiction.

The book is not that, however. Its value lies in its fundamental truth: a truth not of fact but of feeling. Here is a set of snapshots, taken with a rather primitive camera, in the hands of a not very skilful operator, who yet knew what pictures were worth going for. He shows us, quite

[1] The late Sir Arthur Elton was kind enough to furnish a list of the fictitious and real names, transcribed from one that had been added to his own copy of the book. It agrees almost completely with one that is included in another copy, subsequently acquired by the Library of the University of Leicester.

convincingly, the initiation of a new railway clerk (Chap. II). He gives us a good sense of the difficulties that constantly appeared in dealing with the customers of the railway, when they were minded to be awkward p. 66. He has something useful to tell us of the economics and management of a station refreshment room: look at his account of the extortion at Didcot (p. 72), including the charge of a penny for a glass of water.

He is at his best in depicting the stationmaster. He treats us to a brief and amusing view of the varieties of the species (pp. 123–24). More seriously, he sets out to display the stationmaster's position in the society of his town or village. We can accept his general account of the matter (pp. 82–4), noting especially his comment that the stationmaster's importance had already declined a little since the fifties and sixties of which he was writing. The railway, he says, was then 'a new thing, and the clerks and stationmasters were for the most part supplied from the middle class of society, and able to hold their own in a gentlemanly way'; whereas, by the late seventies, they were more and more apt to be 'the descendants of the porters and policemen'. This social change was a consequence of the growth of the railway service itself: a service in which, as it has often been remarked, whole families came to engage. Some allowance must be made here for Simmons's own self-importance; but anybody inclined to lay much stress on that should turn to his report of his conversation with the Rev. Mr Fearnone (the name might have come from Bunyan), in which that admirable clergyman descants on the moral position of the stationmaster (pp. 39–40).

Again, Simmons has some pertinent comments to make on the training and the duties of engine-drivers (pp. 61–64), sharpened by the final anecdote from the footplate of a special train conveying Disraeli and some of his colleagues ('the Queen's minstrels', as the driver calls them) from London to Windsor. And, scattered all through, are entirely convincing pictures of the hardships of railway life: the icy conditions of the primitive signal-box, for example, with the quaint expedient adopted by one signalman for alleviating them (pp. 31–32); the sudden snowstorm and the breakdown of the engine at night between Reading and Twyford (pp. 117–20).

The book is not concerned exclusively with the running of trains. Simmons's snapshots include a gallery of characters: simple country folk like Farmer John, bemused by the telegraph (pp. 57–59), and the poor old woman terrified by her first railway journey (pp. 94–97); Mad Sandy, the rip-roaring driver (pp. 100–03, 151–53). He reveals something of the close rivalry between his own company and the London & North Western in canvassing for traffic (pp. 130–33); and he shows us the daily life of the localities in which he worked, particularly at Thame in Chapter VII and at Bilston in the two concluding chapters of this volume. Here we see the Berkshire farmer's son shying away—can we wonder?—from the barbarities of the Black Country (pp. 138, 159).

Simple and unsophisticated as it is, the book has its own contribution to make to our view of mid-Victorian society and of the place taken in it by the railway, then arriving at the plenitude of its power. A good many other more serious contributions were being made at the same time: general discussions;[1] the careful observations of foreigners;[2] histories of companies;[3] biographies of engineers and contractors;[4] technical descriptions;[5] hints for travellers, including at least one systematic attempt to guide them through the puzzles and dangers of the journey.[6] Michael Reynolds's *Engine-driving Life* (1881) was a spirited attempt to describe the driver's craft; but it remained unique. There were one or two other factual descriptions of the structure of employment: W. F. Mills's book *The Railway Service* (1867) and the *Handbook Guide to Railway Situations*, which Messrs Cassell thought it worth while to add in 1861 to a shilling series they published.[7]

*Ernest Struggles* is an impish supplement to all these solemn works. It was little noticed on its appearance, though the first volume must have sold well enough, in a modest way, to justify the publication of the second. It was sharply criticized in Thomas Cook's *Excursionist*, as Simmons notes in the preface to his second volume. He himself had by this time gone back to the land. He was farming at Caversham, across the river from Reading. He wrote another book, *Stubble Farm: or, Three Generations of Farmers*, which appeared in 1880, as well as two novels, published in 1882 and 1890. He died on 6 December 1895.[8]

---

[1] W. B. Adams, *Roads and Rails* (1862); C. P. Roney, *Rambles on Railways* (1868).

[2] A. C. Franquet de Franqueville, *Du régime des travaux publics en Angleterre* (1874); E. Malezieux, *Les chemins de fer anglais en 1873* (1974); G. Cohn, *Untersuchungen über die englische Eisenbahnpolitik* (1874–75).

[3] J. S. Jeans, *Jubilee Memorial of the Railway System: a History of the Stockton & Darlington Railway* (1875); L. H. Ruegg, *The History of a Railway* (the Salisbury & Yeovil Company) (1878); F. S. Williams, *The Midland Railway* [1876].

[4] C. J. Vignoles, *Life of Charles Blacker Vignoles* (1889): A. Helps, *Life and Labours of Mr Brassey* (1872; reprinted 1970).

[5] Z. Colburn, *Locomotive Engineering and the Mechanism of Railways* (1871); D. K. Clark, *Railway Machinery* (1855), and *Railway Locomotives* (1860).

[6] *The Railway Traveller's Handy Book* (1862; reprinted 1971).

[7] Among modern works that are useful as a commentary on Simmons's account, the most important is P. W. Kingsford, *Victorian Railwaymen* (1971).

[8] Assuming—what seems clear enough—that he can be identified with the Hubert Simmons, farmer, of Portobello Farm, Watlington, who died on that day intestate, leaving £407.

Such little notice as his book had enjoyed soon perished. It has seldom been remembered in the twentieth century. It is not noticed by E. T. MacDermot in his fine *History of the Great Western Railway:* unhappily, for he might well have had something interesting to say of it. The book achieves an improbable reference in a footnote to the history of *The Times*,[1] where it is quoted to illustrate the rivalry between that paper and the *Morning Herald*. For the rest, it has slipped into oblivion. It surely deserves resurrection now.

J.S.

## EDITOR'S NOTE

THE first volume of *Ernest Struggles* is reprinted here complete. A few misprints and obvious errors have been silently corrected. A key to the persons and places mentioned under fictitious names appears on the next page.

If the demand for this first volume is satisfactory, the publishers intend to reissue the second.

The University, Leicester
3 April 1973

[1] *History of The Times*, ii (1939), 84n.

## KEY TO PLACES AND CHARACTERS

(as given in old copies of the book)

*Place Names*

| | |
|---|---|
| Benley | Henley |
| Byfield | Twyford |
| Fame | Thame |
| Fitzboro' | Princes Risborough |
| Grain Road | Challow, formerly Faringdon Rd. |
| Hinoe | Aynho |
| Jam Junction | Reading |
| Plough | Slough |
| Puzzle Junction | Didcot |
| Snorum | Reading or Oxford (certainly Oxford—*ed.*) |
| Wilderness Road | Wantage Road (in fact Wallingford Road, see pp. 23, 65, 66—*ed.*) |

*People*

| | |
|---|---|
| Badger(jr.) | A. Higgins, Supt., London Div. |
| Badger (sr.) | J. D. Higgins |
| Insp. Bull | Insp. Noble |
| Gabriel Gouge | Sir Daniel Gooch |
| Justice | G. N. Tyrrell |
| Levant | Besant |
| McLion | J. Grierson |
| Mulberry | J. Peach, afterwards Div. Supt., Penzance |
| O'Reilly | J. Kelley |
| Sprigalilly | C. E. Spagnoletti |

# Ernest Struggles;

OR THE

COMIC INCIDENTS AND ANXIOUS MOMENTS

IN CONNECTION WITH

# The Life of a Station Master.

BY ONE WHO ENDURED IT.

Reading:
PUBLISHED BY J. J. BEECROFT, MARKET PLACE.

1879.

# PREFACE

Fifteen years' service on the line has furnished me with incidents, the recital of which will, I trust, not only serve to interest my readers, but also tend to throw some light upon railway management.

In spite of the rapid strides which the last fifty years have witnessed in connection with our iron highways, we must not be supposed to have arrived at maturity with our Railways. The mention of the name is suggestive of rapid progress, and the next few years will see changes, of which the past generation—the inventors and early promoters of Railways—never dreamed, and reforms which can only be developed as the system progresses.

The next generation will smile at the amusement furnished by a record of things as they are, for they will doubtless appear as absurd to them as the foolish notions which actuated our fathers, in their opposition to the formation of railways, do to us.

In the meantime the subject is one of *vital* interest to every traveller; and where is the man, woman, or child who is not a traveller? Life is dear to us all; and the Railway Directors who fail to take the necessary precautions against the repetition of accidents—or who, for the sake of *reducing expenditure*, employ an inexperienced staff—need not be surprised that Shareholders will clamour for reform, or that the government will interfere, to compel them to protect life and property.

I do not attribute any intentional neglect to Railway Directors or Managers; much less to Shareholders, who know little or nothing of the practical working of Railways; but I wish clearly to place before them incidents founded on facts, from which probably may arise a practical issue.

Are there not Accidents which are fairly recognized amongst Railway men as *Preventable?* and if so, why do they continually occur?

How is it that *upon principle* claims for compensation are resisted by the Companies? Are not pounds squandered in red-tapism when shillings would satisfy the aggrieved?

Shareholders have a right to ask why their dividends are small; and, if by the following pages, they see how the *gnats* are strained out, and the *camels* swallowed, these chapters will not have been written in vain.

E. S.

## CONTENTS

## CHAPTER VII



## CHAPTER VIII



## CHAPTER IX



## CHAPTER X

## CHAPTER I

*Application for Appointment—Introduction to the Board Room—The Terminus and its Offices—An Excited Clergyman and the Porter—The First Step in Railway Life—'Dido'*

'ERNEST', said my mother, 'I have received a letter from your cousin in the Bedford Road. He is a solicitor, and I have been corresponding with him to obtain you a more lucrative appointment. You are to be at his office at eleven o'clock to-day, so you had better go round to Mr Goodfellow's and ask him to excuse you.'

At that time we were living in the Harrow Road, in a small house. My father had been a large farmer but he was then bankrupt, and being under the process of a lawyer's whitewash, he was living in London in order, more conveniently, to attend the Bankruptcy Court, and was subsisting on the benevolence of his relatives. I had held a situation as farm bailiff in the neighbourhood where my father had been farming, but the great alteration in the position of my parents had weighed heavily on my mind, and I readily embraced an offer to come to London to seek employment amongst strangers.

In half-an-hour's time I entered the office of Mr Goodfellow, a house agent in the Kilburn Road. He could not well refuse my request, as he paid me by commissions only on the rents collected from a street inhabited by the lowest class of Irish, but he hoped I should return at the usual hour in the morning.

I cannot well pass over my short apprenticeship as a London house agent's clerk, without a vivid recollection of those awful Irish, and the threats I had to employ to obtain their weekly rents, not forgetting the heavenly *blessings* that they showered on my head when, as soon as I was directed, I took an inventory of their furniture if the rent were two weeks in arrear.

The most pleasing part of my duty was driving Mr Goodfellow round the St. John's Wood portion of his collection, and although I had to wait a very long time in some instances for him, there was much to interest me in the novelties of London traffic, and the management of his pretty, skittish, little pony.

Ten years after that morning I went to call on Mr Goodfellow and to report my progress in the world, but the poor man was dead, the number of the house and the name of the house agent were altered, and the place knew him no more.

At eleven o'clock on the morning in question I presented myself at the office of my second cousin. He was a thorough London lawyer, and looked as sharp as a two-edged sword. Very few words were wasted in enquiry as to the health of my parents, and in five minutes he had possessed himself of the following information, viz:—That I was twenty years of age, six feet high, could translate fifty lines of Ovid, speak French, carry a sack of beans, break a horse, and write a tolerable hand.

'Now', said he, 'I know what you are just cut out for. I manage the affairs of two gentlemen who are large railway shareholders and are also directors, and I have no doubt that either of them will give me a nomination. I can then get you on as a railway clerk and if you are steady and persevering there is no doubt you will obtain advancement, and you may become a station master. These gentlemen are connected with the London and Cheetem Railway[1] and the Great Smash Railway.[2] Which do you think you would prefer?'

Now, the Great Smash Railway ran through my father's late farm, and as my mother had told me that the object of which I had first taken notice was a train passing the old farm-house, and as my father had told me so many tales in connection with the navvies and those who made the railway through his farm, I at once decided in its favour, and in a very brief space of time I was provided with a letter addressed to A. K. Butcher, Esq., Board Room, Great Smash Terminus, London, which, I was told, would do to make up the number of my testimonials.

'There'! said my cousin, handing me the letters, 'that is the best I can do for you. You had better take this letter at once to Mr Butcher, and he will tell you what to do. You may have to run down to get a testimonial from the Parson of the village where you lived, and a line from the farmer with whom you lived as bailiff; but, perhaps, the house agent's reference

---

[1] The London Chatham & Dover Railway.

[2] The Great Western Railway. This offensive epithet would not have been particularly appropriate in the 1860s, but it made sense when Simmons was writing. In the eight years 1866–73 there had been only one fatal casualty on a Great Western passenger train. But in 1874 there were three bad accidents, at West Drayton, Merthyr, and Shipton-on-Cherwell. The last of these, on Christmas Eve, was the worst that had ever occurred on the British railways.

will do instead. However, here is a sovereign for you in case you want it, and as I have two clients waiting to see me, I must wish you good morning. Give my kind regards to your mother, and tell your father that as his estate shows 15s in the £, he was ill advised to file a petition.'

So saying, he shook hands and opened the door for me simultaneously, and with a hasty glance at his clients, who were pacing the lobby, one with arms folded and the other scratching his head violently, I passed into the street.

Looking at my watch I found it was only 11.30. It seemed to me impossible that such a multitude of things could have been arranged in such a brief space of time, and it was not until I had compared my watch with some clocks in a jeweller's shop that I could persuade myself that it had not stopped.

I made enquiry of a policeman as to the whereabouts of the Great Smash Terminus, and finding I should lose much time in going home, I determined at once to proceed to deliver my letter.

It was with trembling steps that I ascended the stone staircase which led to the board room at the terminus. My timid knock at the door was answered by a stout, good-natured looking man, dressed in a black, tight-fitting coat, with a row of buttons up the centre.

'Who do you want to see, young man' ? enquired the doorkeeper.

I handed him the letter addressed to Mr Butcher, and was directed to take a seat in the passage outside, as the directors were taking their luncheon, and would not be out for at least a quarter of an hour. Whilst I was sitting in the passage some very nice little grills passed in, and sundry bottles of stout, soda water, &c., and the sight made me feel quite hungry. I hoped that my good-natured friend would ask me to partake, but although I could catch sight of him putting a nice kidney and potato out of sight, he took no further notice of me until he summoned me to follow him to the presence of Mr Butcher.

Mr Butcher was reading my cousin's letter of introduction, and appeared to be somewhat amused at its contents. He addressed me in French, and having satisfied himself that I was tolerably proficient in that language, he enquired in English if I could really carry a sack of beans. This also amused the gentleman who was with him, who I afterwards discovered to be Mr Badger, the assistant secretary,[1] and at Mr Butcher's request he undertook to instruct me as to the necessary preliminaries for appointment.

I was directed to wait outside for Mr Badger. He soon joined me, and after I had accompanied him to a very snug office and signed a form of

---

[1] J. D. Higgins.

application in which there was a clause which provided that nothing should be claimed in case I was killed, he informed me that the next day was Board day for the appointment of clerks, and that as Mr Butcher had told him I was anxious to get on the railway at once, I should lose no time in obtaining the necessary testimonials, amongst which should be one from a clergyman who had known me. I undertook to obtain them, and hurried back to my parents to inform them of my success.

Matters discussed, it was decided that I should go down that evening, sleep in the country, and return by first train in time for the directors' meeting. Time permitting, I wrote the letter of application which I was instructed to hand in with the testimonials, and at nine o'clock that evening I presented myself at the house of the clergyman in whose parish I had been reared.

It was perfectly natural for me to call on this gentleman, for in days of prosperity we had been on terms of great intimacy. My father had been Churchwarden for many years, my sister had given her services at the Sunday school, and my mother had assisted with all matters of parish relief, even beyond her means. I had no difficulty in obtaining the testimonial, and on my way to the station in the morning I obtained a satisfactory reference from the farmer I had served as bailiff.

Thus equipped, I presented myself at the Board room of the Great Smash Railway at eleven o'clock precisely. It was a very busy day at the London terminus, and I soon learnt that applicants for appointment would not be seen until all the Board cases had been disposed of.

I forgot to mention that my cousin, the solicitor, had given me the name of a former clerk of his, who was at that time employed at the terminus, and finding I had sufficient time, I determined to seek him. I had to enquire of several before I could ascertain in which office he was employed, but at last I ascertained from a boy messenger, who was running about with a double handful of unstamped letters in yellow envelopes, that he was engaged in the accountants' office, and he directed me thither.

I was never more astonished than when I opened the door to this office. It was like an immense school-room, only that the boys had whiskers and most of them were out at elbows, and all looked miserably thin; moreover, they were all standing to write, and the bundles of papers before each were enough to turn each poor fellow's heart sick. At the head of the table sat a deformed gentleman of about fifty years of age, who I afterwards learnt was Mr Fretsum, the chief accountant.[1] He had gained

[1] William Wood.

his position by steady application; had worked himself up from being an ordinary clerk, and had joined the railway from its commencement. He always came to business at 8.45 a.m. and never left until 6 p.m., and invariably subsisted on a biscuit and a glass of water during the day, ridiculing the idea of the waste of time for dinner. Poor man, the outside world had no charms for him, so he had devoted his life to his office, and was then in receipt of an income much in excess of his requirements. Many of the poorest of the clerks, from necessity's sake, followed his example, and when the clock struck One they quietly pulled out their drawer and ate a piece of dry bread and cheese; but the majority hurried off to a cheap dining room in the neighbourhood.

As I stood waiting to be attended to, I shuddered at the idea of being one of those clerks, and determined that I would rather be a ploughman than a half-starved clerk of this kind.

At last some one asked me what I wanted, and the clerk whom I was seeking came forward. I handed him my cousin's card, and he instructed me to wait outside the Board room, as he was coming there almost directly with some papers which had reference to a station master's accounts, who, as he described it, was 'up before the Board.'

All was bustle and confusion at that mighty station. It was so different from what I had been used to, that I was well nigh bewildered. The station itself was an immense glass house, and as I stood on the balcony outside the Board room, I could command a view of the departing trains below, and hear much that transpired. An express train was loading, and the various railway officials and passengers were as the flies on a summer's day. There was a gentleman in plain clothes who was pointed out to me as the station master, who was anxiously going about, with an occasional glance at his watch. There were two inspectors in livery and buttons, who, with their chests padded after the fashion of the Life Guards, and a flower in their button-hole, were twirling carriage keys and parading the platform, occasionally touching their caps to anyone who looked better dressed than the majority of the passengers; beyond which I failed to see that they did anything. There were the guards of the train, who were alternately stowing away luggage, parcels, and passengers, and who appeared to be most polite to well-dressed people who travelled first class. There were the porters, who brought in the luggage from the cabs, and who never failed to hunt out the owner and to assure him that the luggage was all right, and touch their caps, which seemed to me a waste of time. There was that dreadful newspaper boy who could not pronounce the name of a single newspaper correctly, and whose din I longed to stop. The man going round with a grease box, to grease the axletrees, at the risk of every lady's dress. The boy with a basket of cakes and small bottles of spirits, and passengers of all kinds and descriptions.

The weather was cold, and there was a porter with a trolly full of steaming footwarmers,[1] but I noticed that he put them in the carriages with the people who were well clad and had wraps of all kinds. A poor woman, who looked very ill, ventured to ask for one, but I heard the porter say it was the last he had, and he wanted it for the Superintendent, who was going down by that train. I could not, however, reconcile that statement with his afterwards placing it in a carriage with a very fat old lady, who was travelling first-class with her maid, a lap dog, and a parrot.

Presently the train moved off, and I was tapped on the shoulder by my friend, the clerk from the accountants' office.

'I am sorry to have been so long', he said, 'but we have a very strong case against that station master, and Mr Fretsom is very anxious that every inaccuracy shall be brought against him.'

At that time I knew nothing about railway inaccuracies, or I might have offered up a prayer for the station master who was about to be tried, but I naturally concluded he must have been a very bad fellow, and dismissed him from my thoughts.

My friend, whose name I had forgotten and whom I never saw after that day, having ascertained that his case against the station master would not come on for some time, then volunteered to take me round the station, and enlighten me as to the various offices, &c.

We peeped into the General Manager's office, the Traffic Superintendent's office, the Secretary's office, the Estate office, the Audit office, the Telegraph office, the Superintendent's office, the Booking office, and the Parcels and Cloak room.

The most amusing of these was, however, the cloak room office, at one end of which was a miscellaneous collection of articles, such as no bazaar ever offered for view. These, he told me, were all 'lost articles,' and that each year there were sufficient things to make a large sale by public auction. There were the most beautiful articles of wearing apparel, portmanteaux, boxes, and umbrellas without number, and my friend informed me that the Company once had a carriage and pair of horses arrive for which they never had an owner, and which were sold by auction. I could not understand

[1] Footwarmers were then very new: they were introduced on the Great Western in 1856, for first-class passengers only. They were not, officially, supposed to be available in the second class until 1870, or the third until 1873. E. T. MacDermot, *History of the Great Western Railway* (1964 ed.), i. 371, 446.

how ladies could be so careless as to leave muffs, sables, shawls, opera glasses, &c., without enquiry for them, but he explained that ladies sometimes travelled short distances whilst their husbands were in the city, and that rather than make a fuss about a lost article they could afford to renew it. This was a mystery to me, but my attention was distracted by our arrival at the London goods shed. Here again were a number of clerks, but they were shabbier and dirtier than the clerks at the audit office, and the desks appeared to be a mass of ink, dirt, and oil. I remarked that the place looked rather rough, and was informed that it was the night office, where the clerks worked all night to make out the invoices of goods going by night trains into the country. There were numbers of pair horse vans loading and unloading, and I could not help contrasting the appearance of the beautiful horses with that of the clerks.

We then made our way back to the Board room, passing on our way the up platform. A train had just arrived, and the porters were busily engaged taking the luggage to an enclosed space, in front of which the letters of the alphabet were arranged, and from which the luggage was distributed in alphabetical order.

The station master was engaged in a violent discussion with a country clergyman, who seemed to have lost all control over himself, and was vociferously demanding to be shown to the Board room. The station master giving up all hope of quieting the clergyman, seeing my friend, enquired if he were going upstairs, and requested him to show the gentleman to the Board room. He undertook to do so, and we all marched in that direction. Fortunately for the clergyman's impatient mood the directors had just returned from luncheon, and he was thus enabled to address them. I took advantage of the opportunity to follow them in, as I thought something terrible must have happened. Addressing the chairman he said—

'I never was more grossly insulted in my life, and if I did not bring the matter instantly before you I should consider myself unworthy of the Church of England!'

'But', said the chairman, 'what is it you have to complain of?'

'Sir', said the clergyman, 'it is no light matter. I am a shareholder in this great company, and I demand nothing less than the man's immediate dismissal. I have taken his number. It is 594, Porter.'

'Send for the man', said the chairman.

In a very short space of time Porter No. 594, stood before the directors, and the complainant was directed to state his case.

'I arrived', said he, 'by the last up train, and on asking this man for my luggage, he told me to go to ——. I can scarcely believe my senses, but I most emphatically state that he said it, and I demand nothing less than his immediate dismissal.'

The directors looked much shocked, and Porter No. 594, was then asked—

'What have you to say in answer to this charge?'

No. 594 then came forward and, scratching his head, said—

'Well, gen'emen, I never meant no harm!'

'Meant no harm'! echoed several of the directors; 'then what *did* you mean?'

'Well, gen'emen, the gent, he comed out of the train, and he says to me, says he, 'Porter, where's my luggage?' and I says, says I, what's your name, sur? and he says 'Lester,' and in course I told him to go to L, and he thought I meant t'other place, and would'nt 'ear no reason.'

The matter thus explained, No. 594 was told to resume his duties; and fearing I should be discovered, I too beat a retreat, but not before I had noticed a faint smile on the faces of many of the directors. The clergyman left hastily, and the usual business of the day was proceeded with. My friend's case came on, and I saw no more of him.

During my absence, two rows of men had been arranged in the passage for appointment in the service, the one row as porters and the other as police. They had all undergone the then usual process of being stripped before the company's doctor, and those who were reported sound in body, 36 inches round the chest, and 5 feet 10 inches in height, were passed in before the directors, who examined their testimonials and antecedents.

In addition to some fifty of these candidates were, like myself, applicants for clerks' situations, some with long beards and eyeglasses, and some beardless youths, one of whom was continually re-writing his letter of application, and I was just getting acquainted with him when my name was called, and I was ushered into a prominent position in the Board-room with a beating heart.

'This', said Mr Badger, the assistant secretary, 'is the young man Mr Butcher has mentioned.'

'Mr Butcher is unavoidably absent to-day, but he has left a letter respecting him.'

Whilst the directors were perusing my testimonials, I took a timid glance round the room which, with its turkey carpet, clean blotting paper, quill pens, and beautiful table, compared favourably with the goods office I last saw, and I was struck with an immense oil-painting of the late secretary, which was suspended at the end of the room. This picture was often referred to as a joke in after life, for when a fellow got into trouble, it had long been said that he was 'going to see the picture.'[1]

Very few words were said to me. I was asked if I should like to 'go on at once,' and as I replied in the affirmative, I was told to go into the next room and it would be arranged. Not a word was said as to what were to be my duties, or as to what my salary was to be, but I waited patiently in the adjoining room until Mr Badger came to me. It was not long before the assistant secretary came in. He was a pleasant-looking man, prematurely bald, with sandy whiskers. Report said he was the son of a country miller, but having been unfortunate in the butter trade, he had originally sought refuge in the Great Smash Railway. If he had not the advantage of a liberal education, constant communication with the directors had wonderfully polished him, and it was also said that he was necessarily acquainted with all the little irregularities connected with the directors' management, which gave him great power. In fact he was confidential clerk to several of them. He was very kind to me, and told me that through the kind mention of Mr Butcher—although there were several appointed clerks on the book who would be called in rotation, probably one or two months hence—I was to go to work immediately. He asked me if I should prefer London or the country, and as I had seen quite enough of the London offices to deter me from wishing to enter one, I decided on the country.

'Very well', said he, 'I see I have an order for a clerk at "Snorum" station,[2] and I will write you a pass for that station, and give you a letter to Mr Peltum, the district superintendent.'

'Will you go to-day?'

'Thank you,' I replied, 'I should like to have time to go home and pack my clothes. If to-morrow will do, I would rather go then.' To-morrow was decided on, and accordingly I trotted home to prepare for to-morrow's journey, and to take leave of my parents. I went round to thank my cousin for the nomination, but he was away on a trial his clerk said, so I left a note for him. My parents were pleased that I had been successful, because I had hitherto been living chiefly on the savings of my boyhood, which amounted to £120 when I left the farm, but which had been reduced in London to £90. Amongst other things of which I was possessed was furniture for a bed and sitting-room, and a black and white spaniel dog, called Dido, I decided to leave the furniture, but to take the dog. As Dido was my faithful companion for some time, you must permit me to describe him to

---

[1] The portrait was that of the former Chairman, Charles Russell, by Sir Francis Grant.

[2] Oxford.

you. He was a medium-sized spaniel, half clumber breed and half water spaniel, more black than white, very long ears, and large eyes. The knowledge bump on his head was very prominent, and he was very quick and active. His father was the old sporting dog to which we had all shot for years, and although not an educated dog, he was never surpassed as a sportsman, and was always backed to catch more rabbits on sporting occasions than any one present should shoot, no matter how many beaters were engaged. I had Dido from a puppy, and during my life as a farm bailiff he was my constant companion, and after five o'clock in the winter evenings he was my only friend. He would never rest as a puppy unless he was learning something, consequently I had taught him many tricks, amongst which—however incredible it may seem—the following were his accomplishments; and my relations called him 'the educated dog':—

He would fight any dog, no matter how large, and although he often got severely bitten, it was no warning to him, but he never took the aggressive part.

He would keep sheep up after the manner of a sheep dog, or keep them away from the troughs whilst their food was put in, and he could even discriminate between the ewes and the lambs, allowing the lambs to pass. Many a time he has been bunted over by an old ewe when he has not been looking out.

He would put the pigs in the yard if they got out. He would keep the fowls out of the garden, and when I wanted to catch a young chicken to kill, he would follow me until he was certain as to which one I wanted, when he would run it down in no time for me, and put his paws upon it without biting it, until I came up.

He would kill rats, but it was always distasteful to him; and although we have been for hours ferreting, without the aid of anyone, he on one side of the hedge and I on the other, he always sneezed and shook his head after killing a rat, as much as to say I don't like it. On these occasions, if the ferret came out of the hole on his side, he immediately came through to me with his tail down, and we exchanged sides. Rabbiting after this fashion he delighted in, and I have seen him keeping himself out of sight of the rabbit about to bolt out of the hole until it came fairly out, when bunny's chance of escape was very slight, but of course it had been a great trouble to teach him to do that, as good dogs are always impetuous.

He was a splendid water dog, and would stick to a moorhen, and even dive after her, until she was obliged to fly, and he never spoilt a bird in retrieving it. He could not open a hedgehog like many dogs, but he would find them repeatedly, and never leave them until I came to relieve him.

He once killed a weasel, but he was very sick after it. Although he killed rats, his mouth was so tender that he would retrieve a hen's egg any distance; and he was under such good command that I have often turned young hares and rabbits down alive in the kitchen at the farmhouse, and he would bring them to me without injuring them in the least. In fact I have known partridges which were knocked down fly away again as he was retrieving them. In addition to these rougher duties, I had taught him to fetch my slippers, ring the bell, by pulling the bell rope, shake hands, beg, jump through a hoop, and play at hide and seek with children. That is to say—you might show him any article, tell him to leave the room, and then call him in to find it. Perhaps his most useful trick was fetching the letters from the turnpike every morning, across a large field. When the postman blew his horn, Dido was off, and in three minutes accomplished a journey which took either of us ten minutes on foot.

Was it to be wondered that when I left the farm-bailiff's situation, I refused £5 of the farmer for my dog; and that I found in him a true and faithful companion. In fact, the dog was not at home without me, and I was not at home without the dog. Therefore I, dog, and baggage trotted off together by an early train on the morrow. It was the first time we had travelled at others expense, and I took advantage of some part of my leisure time to examine the pass, which said—

*Pass* Mr Ernest Struggles

from

*London to Snorum.*

and then came—

Why granted, 'Clerk on Probation.'

On the back of it was also printed a paragraph repudiating the Company's responsibility in case I was killed by accident.

I had begun to feel quite grand with my second-class free pass, but what with the 'Clerk on Probation' and the continually signing or reading something about being killed, I indulged in sundry reflections as the train came in sight of the dear old farm where I was born and reared.

It was about midway between London and Snorum stations, and oh, how I wished my dear father and mother were again at the old farm, and how a thousand sweet memories flashed through my mind, and before we were out of sight of the elm trees I had so often climbed, the tears were coursing down my cheeks, and but that I noticed they had attracted the observation of my opposite fellow-passenger, I could have wept aloud. Beyond my dog now and then popping his head from under the seat and licking my hand during the journey, I had no converse or sympathy with any one, and I was glad when the train arrived at Snorum.

## CHAPTER II

*Snorum—Mr Peltum—Joe War—Our Landlady—The Goods Office—The 'British Public'—The 'Lion'—A Fracas—Re-appointment*

TYING Dido to one of my boxes, and seeking my letter of introduction to Mr Peltum, I enquired for his office, and was very soon standing respectfully before him awaiting his instructions.

He was a gentleman of about fifty years of age, short and thin, and he wore spectacles and very long brown hair, which hung in ringlets over his shoulders and down his back. He could not sound the letter *r*, but always made *w* of it, and you could never tell whether he were looking at you or not, as he had a way of turning his head and looking sideways. His brother being a clergyman, it was supposed that he too was an educated man, and he was able to cast three columns of figures, viz., £ s d, simultaneously.

He read Mr Badger's letter, and then asked me what family Mr Butcher, the director, had.

This question was undoubtedly put to me in order that Mr Peltum might ascertain to what extent Mr Butcher, the director, took an interest in me, as Mr Badger had doubtless mentioned his nomination in the letter I had delivered.

I unsuspectingly replied that I did not know Mr Butcher, and that my cousin was his solicitor. Mr Peltum then told me that I should have to assist in the goods office at Snorum for a short time, but that I must not consider that my ultimate destination as he had other views for me. He then gave me a letter to Mr White, the goods manager at Snorum, and told me to enquire of Mr War, the booking clerk, as to lodgings.

I sought Mr War. He was in the booking office booking some numbers from the tickets.

He surveyed me from head to foot after I had told him my mission, and then said—'To begin with, don't call me Mr War. My name is "Joe." If you want lodgings, I dare say they can take you in at my crib. I am just going home to dinner, and you had better come along with me.'

Joe War was rather a pleasing looking young man of from 22 to 23 years of age. He was tall and dark, with no whisker, and a very slight moustache.

He parted his hair down the middle, and but for his complexion being very sallow, and his mouth being cut out of the straight, he would have been a handsome fellow. He dressed very fashionably, wore a red neck tie, and cocked his hat a little on one side, which seemed to counteract the expression of his mouth.

'What do you wear those awful deerstalker hats for', said Joe. 'I always wear a top hat in the town. It's no good being poor and looking poor. Always keep yourself up. That's my motto.'

I told him that I had a top hat amongst my luggage, but that I usually wore it on Sundays only, as it seemed always in the way.

'That's not a bad sort of dog of yours', said Joe.

By this time we had arrived at the lodgings, and it was soon arranged that another bed should be put in Joe's room, and that we should share the expense of living, and take our meals together, commencing at once.

Our landlady, or housekeeper, was a widow, about fifty years of age, whose husband had been killed on the line, and I soon ascertained that she was indebted almost entirely to Joe War for her living. She was a very meek kind of woman, who never put herself out about trifles. Joe's meals were always ready at the time appointed if he liked to come for them, and his latch key admitted him at all hours, without check or remonstrance from his landlady, who always retired to rest after she had spread the supper.

Dinner over, Joe had to return to book the passengers for an up train, and I proceeded to present myself to Mr White, the goods agent.

Mr White was an elderly gentleman who had the air of a retired sea captain. He wore a suit of plaid clothes, and looked like what is commonly called a 'good sort of man.' All went well until he elicited from me the fact that I knew nothing of railway work, when he said something about sending him useless humbugs. I felt my colour coming, and was about to reply, when he apologized to me for having allowed such an observation to escape his lips, and went on to say that had I but known the number of new clerks that that old teetotal humbug Peltum had sent him during the last three years who knew nothing, and then removed them when he had hammered it into them, he was sure I should sympathize with him.

'Why', said he, 'if it was not for two pauper-boy supernumeraries that can't get appointed—and here he chuckled to himself—I should never get my monthly accounts in, or keep the work going.'

'But there, young man', said he, putting his hand on my shoulder, 'don't let me dishearten you. You come in the morning at nine o'clock and we will do the best we can with you. It is only the old game over again to us.'

That afternoon and evening I employed myself by taking a walk round the town, unpacking my things, and assisting the landlady at our lodgings to put up an iron bedstead she had hired for my use.

Joe, the booking clerk, did not come home until I had been asleep for some time, and possibly I should not then have heard him had not Dido, who insisted on sleeping under my bed, forbidden his coming into the room, and his growling and barking awoke me.

Joe was rather cross about it, and I was obliged to conciliate him and make the dog lie outside on the mat. He was off at 7.0 a.m. to book the first train, so we got up together, and I took a nice walk outside the town before breakfast.

It was a great relief to me to be again in the country, and Dido enjoyed a hunt for a moorhen alongside the river. The prospect of again earning my living was also cheering, and I tied Dido up and went to the goods office a little before 9 o'clock. The two supernumerary boy clerks before mentioned by Mr White had been there at work since 8 o'clock. They were shabbily dressed, but knew all about the work. One dealt with goods inwards, and the other with goods outwards.

The 'inwards' clerk had already collected the invoices of goods which had arrived during the night with various goods, and had tied them neatly together, making quite a little book without a cover. He addressed himself to me, and I soon found out that I was to belong to the 'inwards.'

Shortly after my arrival two other clerks came in, and then Mr Brown, the chief clerk, as they called him, followed by Mr White. Mr Brown wore a black frock coat, several rings, and had the appearance of a dancing master. I soon found out that he assumed the position of chief, for after the letters had been opened and Mr White had dictated a few letters to Mr Brown, which the latter took down in shorthand, Mr White took his departure ostensibly to settle claims and canvass for traffic. All the work was to me like so much Greek. I looked over the clerks' shoulders, but there was nothing I could understand.

'I see you are doing nothing', said Mr Brown to me. 'The checker is ill this morning, so you had better take these invoices and check off the goods.'

So saying, he handed me the bundle which the supernumerary lad clerk had collected.

'You should find all these goods in trucks, either in the goods shed or in the yard', continued Mr Brown, 'and it will give you an insight. When you find the goods, make a mark √ so, but if they are not there, make a cross, × so, against the entry, and then come in the office and write to the sending station, reporting them, "Not to hand."'

I took the bundle of invoices and a new pencil quite cheerfully, and left the office with the intention of ticking them off in first-class style.

The first invoice was from London. It was a large one with quite 100 entries on it; but what was my disappointment when I found I could not read it. I took it round a corner and sat on an empty barrel, but it was no good, as with one exception there was not a single word written in full, and that was 1 flat, which I mentally ejaculated must mean myself. The other entries were:—

| | which I afterwards learnt meant |
|---|---|
| 1 p. pcl. ... ... ... ... ... ... ... ... | 1 paper parcel. |
| 1 ety. ck. ... ... ... ... ... ... ... | 1 empty cask. |
| 1 pcl. dpy. ... ... ... ... ... ... ... | 1 parcel drapery. |
| 1 tce. gcy. ... ... ... ... ... ... ... | 1 tierce grocery. |
| 1 hd. syp. ... ... ... ... ... ... ... | 1 hogshead syrup. |
| 1 ck. D.S.Y. ... ... ... ... ... ... ... | 1 cask dry saltery. |
| 1 ck. Vgr. ... ... ... ... ... ... ... | 1 cask vinegar. |
| 1 bx. btr. ... ... ... ... ... ... ... | 1 box butter. |
| &c., &c. | |

On the invoice were marks of grease and ink, and I at once recognized the dreadful writing and the general appearance as being true characteristics of the office I had so recently visited in London.

I gave it up as a bad job, and turning it over I found the next invoice to be something that I could deal with, and my hopes brightened as I read aloud—

| | Tons. | cwt. |
|---|---|---|
| 1 truck pigs ... ... ... ... ... ... ... ... ... | 4 | 10 |

It struck me as being rather odd that these pigs should be weighed alive, because when, in my farming days, I despatched sheep to the London market, I had to pay for a truck or half a truck according to number, and irrespective of weight, but I went in search of them, and I fully expected to hear them grunting.

They were not in the goods shed, so I looked elsewhere, and one at a time I climbed up the twelve trucks that were standing outside, in search of the pigs, but nowhere could I find them. I had begun to despair, and was just going to write, 'Not to hand' on the invoice, when I saw the number of the truck marked on the invoice, and I renewed my search. I found the truck, but when I climbed again to look for the pigs, I found it was full of long pieces of moulded stuff, which certainly was not pigs or food for pigs.

Never since that time have I seen a bar of pig iron but it has reminded me of my early ignorance of that article. So I marked the pigs, 'Not to hand', and turned to the next invoice.

Here, for the first time, I found an article, viz., one ladder; for there was the ladder on the top of a truck load of building materials, but the next entry, 'one monkey', was nowhere. I looked in the covered trucks and I looked in the open ones, and thinking that a monkey would be sure to attract the attention of the porters, I went and enquired if they had seen it.

The men set up a laugh, of which I failed to see the joke, and with a scarlet face I repaired to the office to seek the assistance of one of the supernumerary clerks.

'I knew', said he, 'that you could not do it when Mr Brown set you at it; but it's no good saying anything to him. Put them down here and help me by casting this cash-book. The other clerks will go to dinner at 12.45, and then I will run round with you. It won't take us long.'

By this means I got through the difficulty, but it took me some days to master the railway abbreviations, and the men were apt to say, 'Have you found that monkey yet, sir?'

I need hardly tell my readers that the monkey was an article used by builders. Little by little I mastered the various books that were kept for the goods inwards, and Mr White began to take an interest in correcting any little errors in my letters of correspondence, and I got quite on friendly terms with him.

As the goods clerks were allowed to have a half holiday on Saturday, with the exception of one clerk who remained to take the money and to invoice out the goods, I had the afternoon at my disposal, and at the invitation of Joe War, I walked up to see him 'book a few passengers in style,' as he called it. As I approached the passenger station, I noticed a large number of cabs plying to and from the station and the town, and I soon ascertained that the pupils from the College were the cause of all the extra traffic, and that the vacation having commenced, they were all hurrying to their homes by train. The booking office was crammed with them, and they were pushing one another in order to get near to the little pigeon hole where the tickets were given out. It was with difficulty that I got to the door of Joe War's office. He did not take any notice of my knocking, so I called him by name, and he let me in, hastily re-closing the door and locking it. Joe was pleased to see me, and he turned up his coat sleeves as if to perform some conjuring trick.

'Now, my boy', said he, 'I will show you a move. That's the British public outside, and I hate them, and this is Joe War, and I'll let 'em know it. Do you see these boots, old man', and so saying, he pulled up his trousers and displayed some spring elastic side boots, which were getting a little shabby, 'and do you see these coins', pointing to two 2s pieces and three shilling coins on the counter. I looked at the coins, for I never saw any just like them before. 'Ha! ha'! said Joe, 'you don't see the joke! Can't you see that they have had a piece nicked out of them. They are duffers! I should like to wring the neck of that cove up in the cashier's office in London. I'll back he is doing a good thing up there. Every now and then he sends me down a 'duffer', which he swears I took and sent to him. I wouldn't care about that if he didn't nick a piece out of the coin, and then he coolly debits my account with the money. I have to send a good coin in place of it, and then he thinks I am going to see myself robbed like that. What's the odds he is not in with a swim of bad coiners and palms their coins off on us country coves! But I am not quite such a fool. If the British public rob me, I mean robbing them; so I have stuck a bit lead in the nicks, and they must all go by this very next train. Just count that cash in my till, will you?'

I counted the cash. There was £2 1s 4d. Joe took out the 1s 4d, put in the bad coins, took out good coins to same value, and by that time the students were clamouring loudly for tickets. The office was quite full of them, and they were thumping the pigeon hole slide violently.

'Now, Mr British public', said Joe, rubbing his hands, 'it wants just seven minutes to the time of train starting, I'll give you gruel'! and so saying he opened the slide for tickets. At least, four hands were thrust into the office through the aperture, and twenty voices were heard asking for tickets to different places. Joe decided on one place first, and calling out that all those who wanted tickets for that place would be served first, Joe proceeded to issue the tickets.

The fare was 7s 11d. Joe handed the ticket, and receiving in most cases half a sovereign, he promptly put down one penny, called out 'nine shillings', and then adding one shilling change, said 'ten', handling out another and another with a sleight of hand that was marvellous.

He had not calculated it right, as 7s 11d, 1d, and 1s only made 9s, and each passenger was thus defrauded of 1s. So I told him of the mistake, but the only reply I got was, 'Shut up, you coon', so I did not interfere further, and indeed I was afraid they would not all get tickets before the train started.

The bell was then ringing to signal its approach, and two passengers had grabbed their tickets and left their change altogether. I am ashamed to say that I don't think a single passenger by that train received his right change. I made several mental calculations between the tickets and the amounts, but they invariably worked out wrong. The train was detained about three minutes, waiting for the passengers to be booked, but it started at last; and when the whistle sounded, Joe closed the window and danced a horn pipe in the centre of the booking office.

'Ernest', said he, for he had commenced to call me by my christian name, 'just look in my cash-drawer and pick me out those "duffer coins." '

I proceeded to hunt amongst huge bowls of silver, but nowhere could I find one.

'Not find one', said Joe. 'Then where can they be?' and he struck up a song about—

' Oh where, oh where is my little dog gone,
Oh where, oh where is he?
With his ears cut short and his tail cut long,
Oh where, oh where can he be?'

'Ernest', said Joe, 'just call off the numbers on the bottoms of those tickets that are standing out, and the names of the stations.'

I did this, and with an alacrity that surprised me, Joe put them down in his train book, and called out the total amount wanted for tickets sold by that train.

'Now Master Ernest', said he, 'count the cash whilst I do a weed', and Joe seated himself before the office fire and lit a good cigar with all the ease of a prince in his drawing-room.

I counted the silver into pounds, and Joe never troubled even to look at me. In fact he was sitting with his back to me. When I had completed, he enquired the amount. It was £2 7s 0d in excess of the amount required, not forgetting the £2 he commenced with. Joe locked the proper amount in the iron safe, kept for the purpose, and adjusting his ticket case pocketed the £2 7s, closed the cash drawer, and said, 'Come on young man.'

Our first call was at the boot shop, where Joe selected a pair of 21s boots, and I then understood his reason for displaying the old ones to me before booking the train. Next he bought a nice cucumber, and then about 4 lbs of salmon, at 1s per lb.

'There, Master Ernest', said Joe, 'I must get back to book the up cheap, but you get our landlady to cook this salmon by 7 o'clock, and we will have a hot tea for once. Why shouldn't we taste salmon as well as the British public?'

I obeyed Joe's instructions, and at the appointed time the salmon was served up with cucumber and melted butter.

'By jove', said Joe, 'I forgot the shrimps; but never mind, hand me some of that "Cocks" sauce. That's the first sauce that ever was bottled, my boy, and the old cock that sells it is an old brick.[1] The other night he went to sleep in the train and came beyond his intended journey. He had his little daughter with him. I think he called her Jessie, and she went to sleep too. The Inspector was going to excess them for coming beyond their journey, but I thought he looked a jolly old chap, so I let him off the excess and took him up to the Lion Hotel. He would make me come and have some wine with him, and then he told me all about this sauce. How his father and mother were butler and housekeeper to an old lady, who left them the receipt when she died. The first sauce they made in a stew pan; but the most amusing part was how his father advertised it. There were no trains in those days, so he went up by road waggon to London and took some sauce with him. He used to call at the roadside inns, where the waggoners had their dinners, and pull out a bottle and give them all a drop, and then give what was left to the landlady. Catch a man doing that now. He puts a thundering great advertisement up with a painting of a sick lion in a net, or a likeness of the Queen to catch the eye, and then rides about first class, and does it all by correspondence.'

After supper, I tendered Joe half the cost of the salmon and cucumber, but he would not take it, and we had an argument.

'Ernest, my boy', said he, 'that's bunce.'

'Bunce', said I, 'What's that?'

'You are green', said Joe. 'Why bunce is makings, Fancy a chap coming straight from a house agent's office in London and not knowing what bunce is.'

'If you don't mind', said I, 'I would much rather pay half.'

Joe buttoned his coat, picked his teeth, and crossing his legs, said—

'Now, young man, I know all about you and why you want to pay half, and I must read you just one lesson. There was a time when I was as squeamish as you, and if anybody left a shilling, I called them back, but that time is dead; and if you think you're going to be on a railway and go straight, I tell you, once for all, you will find your mistake out. Why, there is old Peltum, the superintendent, and that Calcraft, the auditor,[2] if they were to catch you £1 short in your cash, they would have you up before the Board the very next Wednesday, and 'sack' is the name for it, straight off. Besides, if a fellow doesn't dress well and keep himself respectable, Peltum would shift him to the goods, and there you can't make a stiver, and must go in rags for the rest of your life. Do you think the Directors imagine for one

[1] Cocks' Sauce was a celebrated product of Reading, first manufactured in 1789.

[2] William Calcraft (1800–79) was executioner to the City of London, and the best-known hangman of his time. Hence Simmons's choice of the pseudonym.

moment that 22s 6d per week keeps me? Not they. They know all about it; and when they appoint booking clerks, they ought to say, 'There's a place for you; we know you can't live on what we pay you, but go in and do the best you can for yourself; but, by George, don't let us catch you."'

Such was Joe's reasoning, and knowing that he would be offended at any further offer to pay half, I did not proffer it, but I secretly determined to eat no more salmon thus obtained.

'Now then', said Joe, 'I am going up to the Lion to put just one sov. on a horse that I fancy for the next race. Come along.' Joe having first put on his new boots, his top hat, and provided himself with a silver-mounted cane, cosmetiqued his moustache, and tucked a new silk-pocket handkerchief half into his side coat pocket.

The waiters all touched their heads, for they had no hats on, to Joe, as he walked into the billiard room of the Lion a recognized swell. There was a bar at one end of it, and young lady with curls, dressed in black silk, was serving the liquors.

'Allow me, Miss Smart, to introduce my young friend, Mr Struggles, to your notice', said Joe, and handing to her a bunch of violets which he had bought of a flower girl in the street for 2d, Joe lazily hung over the counter.

Miss Smart half nodded and half bowed to me.

'My young friend has not been about much, Miss Smart', continued Joe, 'although he has lived in London. Don't you think he is in very good hands?'

'*Very*,' said Miss Smart, with a decided stress on the word.

'By the bye, Miss Smart, has Joe Hobbs, the bookmaker, been in?'

Joe Hobbs had not been in, but he was expected, and he very soon came in and registered Joe's bet at 25 to 1, and the remaining sovereign of the £2 7s 0d left his pocket for ever.

'Mr War', said Miss Smart, 'who is that man with the red face playing at billiards. He has been abusing the Railway Company fearfully. Says he went by a train to-day when the students were going home. That they never opened the window of the booking office until seven minutes before the train started, and that then he was docked 1s in his change, and had to run for his life to get into the train, and nearly fell between the train and the platform in getting in. He talks of calling on Mr Peltum in the morning to complain.'

'Does he', said Joe, clenching his teeth. 'I don't know the cad'; and he then muttered to himself, 'All right, Mr British Public; go ahead, but mind how you start.'

The man with the red face was losing his game, and, throwing down the cue, said to his opponent, 'I'm out of form. I got upset this afternoon at the station, and I've not been myself since.'

So saying, he put his coat on, and taking a bamboo-looking walking stick was preparing to leave, when he for the first time confronted me.

'If I mistake not', said he, 'you are the young man who swindled me out of a shilling in my change at the station to-day. I hope it may do you good; but I intend to call on Mr Peltum's brother, the Rev. Mr Peltum, in the morning, and if I can get you dismissed, you may rely on my doing my best.

I assured him that he was mistaken, for although I might have been in the office, I had never booked any one. My assertion was disputed, and I began to feel myself in a very awkward position.

Joe War hastily took off his gold watch and chain, and handing it together with his purse and cane to Miss Smart, he adjusted a large ring on the third finger of his right hand, and strode up to the stranger before I had time to say more.

'Now, Mr red face', said Joe, 'you have made an assertion in a public room before all these gentlemen. If you had a particle of good breeding about you, you would not have done such a thing, but would have written or gone to Peltum. Now I happen to know that this young man, pointing to me, has never booked a passenger in his life, and unless you apologize to him before I count three, you shall have what you deserve.'

'Apologize!' said the man with the red face. 'I swear he was the clerk I saw in the office when I took my ticket.'

'One', said Joe.

'Pretty thing indeed; first to be robbed, and then to have to apologize to the clerk who robs you.'

'Two', said Joe.

'If it was a mistake, I suppose it was; but I don't think so.'

'Three', said Joe, and in a moment he had struck his opponent between the eyes, and he was on his back, and the blood was streaming from a gash in his face close to his eye, caused by Joe's ring. The red-faced stranger got up and made a rush at Joe, but he placed his head in chancery and pummelled his face until he was a mass of blood and bruises. Some of the company separated them, and called out for time. Joe waited for him, and floored him each time with a knock down blow. The company persuaded him to stop, but Joe declared he would not stop until he apologized. The stranger then rushed for his stick, and unsheathing a long dagger was preparing to rush at Joe. The company suddenly cleared away from him, but a sudden impulse seized me, and with a desperate effort I seized the dagger and wrested it from his grasp. A stout, strong man, about 6ft. 2in., who had been a non-commissioned officer in the Life Guards, then stepped up to me, and requested that I would hand him the sword stick. He re-sheathed it, and, breaking it into two pieces across his knee, thrust it into the fire. At this moment some one who knew the red-faced man came in, and with some persuasion took him away.

Joe retired to the lavatory, had a good wash in cold water, brushed his hair and clothes, reclaimed his watch and purse from Miss Smart, and in five minutes time was quietly sitting smoking a weed, the admired champion of the room. Miss Smart called him a very naughty man, but she found him a little piece of sticking plaster for one of his knuckles; beyond which he came out of the affray without a scratch.

'Ernest', said Joe, 'I guess Mr British Public won't turn up to complain to the Rev. Mr Peltum in the morning, neither will he take those black eyes to church.'

The fight and the sword-stick had quite upset me, and I scarcely recollect what reply I made, but I was thankful that matters were no worse, and very glad, indeed, when Joe made up his mind to go home.

That night I had some dreadful dreams about booking passengers and fighting, and I thought we were all at school again, and that the master had punished us by setting us a copy to write out 1,000 times, and that copy was 'Honesty is the best policy.'

Despite Joe's ridicule of the Goods' Office and 'no bunce', it was very comforting to me to work quietly away there at the Inwards Goods. Mr White was getting quite confidential with me, and at the end of the month of probation he sent in a favourable report, and I was appointed at a salary of £60 per annum. A week later Mr Peltum sent for me to his office.

'Mr Stwuggles' (r pronounced as w), said Mr Peltum, 'I told you that your appointment would be only tempowawy. Mr O'Wiley (O'Reilly) the Superintendent of the line,[1] and myself contemplate an awangement, and in the event of that awangement being cawied out, you will have to go to Wilderness Woad (Road)[2] as booking Clerk.'

I enquired if there would be any increase of salary for the removal, but Mr Peltum said not, and that if I did not wish to stand in my own light I had

[1] James Kelley. He was Superintendent of the Northern Division of the G.W.R. 1855–60. The Superintendent of the Line at this time was C. A. Saunders, who did not retire until 1863.

[2] 'Wilderness Road' is the equivalent of the station now know as Cholsey & Moulsford, but then situated three-quarters of a mile nearer London, on the road from Streatley to Wallingford. 'Wilderness' is Wallingford.

better make no objection to an awangement which was made for my benefit.

I was to go on the following Monday. I felt sorry to leave Mr White, and he tried to persuade me to stop, but I did not like to offend Mr Peltum; and accordingly on the following Monday I packed up, took leave of Joe, and applied for the necessary pass from Mr Peltum.

'In sending you to Wilderness Woad', said Mr Peltum, 'I have to say that I only wish I was sending you as a teetotaller, but although I have no case in point *as yet*', and he laid stress on as yet, 'against the station master at that station, I have evewy weason to believe that he lives too fweely, and I caution you not to follow his example.'

As the train started, Joe rushed out to shake hands with me, and as a parting instruction he shouted out, 'Whatever you do, old man, be down upon the British public. You'll find 'em out now. Let 'em have it. Don't spare 'em. Good-bye, old boy.'

## CHAPTER III

*Wilderness Road—The Inn and its Landlords—The Station Master—The Telegraph—Sheep Fair—Dido in request—The Signal Box—Mr Calcraft, the Auditor—A Foggy Night, and its Experiences—Rev. Mr Fearnone*

WILDERNESS Road was a roadside station 17 miles from Snorum. It was the nearest station to the town of Wilderness, a country market town from which it was distant 3 miles. The station was in a very bleak, exposed position, quite small, and the booking office and waiting room were combined, as a low open counter was the only distinction, and one fireplace served for the whole. Mr Milsom was the station master. He was a nice looking man, only his whiskers and beard were of a reddish colour, and contrasted quite ridiculously with a yellow curled wig, for he had no natural hair on the upper portion of his head.

After a careful perusal of my letter of introduction, Mr Milsom suggested that I should accompany him to the Station Hotel opposite, which he told me was the only place I could lodge at, and we adjourned thither. The hotel was that day changing hands, and the late landlord stood on the steps at the entrance, he having just completed the transfer to the new people. He appeared to be on most familiar terms with Mr Milsom, who addressed him as follows:—

'Well, Mr late landlord, so you have pulled it off this time?'

'Yes', said the retiring proprietor, 'its planted this time, and I have just drawn my £200 good-will; but of course, Mr Milsom, 'taint all profit, for what with the getting of it up and the keeping of it up until the inventory is settled, it runs into some money; but there's one thing, this one can't back out like them tother two did.'

'But', said Mr Milsom, 'they both forfeited the deposit, and you must have cleared at least £40 each time.'

'No, no', interrupted the landlord, 'the auctioneer stuck to half each time for his expenses, and then you see what the "getting of it up" cost. Why, if you recollect, one on 'em stopped here four days, and I can assure you, Mr Milsom, I spent near upon £3 in what I gave away outside for to be sent for in beer whilst he was a stopping here to see the trade, just for to keep it lively, and it's no go if you don't; and now, continued he, I'll be bound as it will cost me £1 a day what I gives away for to be drunk whilst I am a waiting about to get the inventory settled, 'cos if I didn't the old chap might cut up nasty, and swear I had done him; but there, come along in, Mr Milsom, and have a glass of summut hot to wet the job.'

We followed him into the bar parlour and seated ourselves on a very comfortable sofa, near the fire, behind a large screen. Mr Milsom's favourite beverage was hot whiskey and water, with lemon and sugar. I had some ale, and the ex-landlord hot rum. Mr and Mrs Finch were the new landlord and landlady. Mr Finch was a gentleman quite sixty years of age, very feeble, his hair quite white, and it did not take five minutes to see that he was very irritable. Mrs Finch was a tall, dark woman, of not more than forty years of age, with black curls and a sallow complexion.

I ordered a bed and what I required, and having no preference for a dark back parlour, which looked out on a water-butt, a pigstye, and a bucket, I took up my position in the bar parlour behind the screen. Mr Milsom and the late landlord were having quite a *tête-à-tête*, and as each customer came to the counter, of which position they commanded a view, I heard the late landlord make the following remarks:—

'That's old Mother Jones' son. I called and left 6d with his mother just now.'

'That's for your railway chaps. I tipped them 2s 6d just as that last train came in.'

'By George, there's a regular customer, and that the first as has been in since we've set here.'

'See a week over, and then see how many they'll have in of a hafternoon. Why I've set in this chair manys a time and gone clean off to sleep, and never a soul's been in.'

Their conversation did not interest me at all, so with Mr Milsom's permission I took a stroll round with Dido to see if we could find private lodgings. I soon discovered that Wilderness road was indeed an isolated place. There was another public house about 300 yards distant and about six cottages of various dimensions, but beyond these, nothing in the shape of human habitation.

I met an old gentleman who looked like a respectable farmer, and he eyed me and my dog very narrowly, and he looked very much inclined to speak, but I was soon satisfied that there was no hope of getting any private lodgings, and accordingly returned to the Station Hotel.

'Some one is enquiring for Mr Milsom', said Mrs Finch, the landlady.

Mr Milsom got up, and as he did so, I could see that the whiskeys and waters were telling upon him. The 'some one' was a neat little servant girl, who had been sent by Mrs Milsom to tell her newly-wedded husband that his dinner had been ready some time, and would he come home?

'Tell Mrs Milsom', said the station master, 'that there's a new clerk come, and that I shan't be home to dinner. I'll have a bit of something with my tea.'

'Please, sir', said the little maid, 'Missus said as I was to tell you as she'd got your favourite for dinner—a beefsteak pudding, and she shouldn't touch it if you didn't come.'

With this Mr Milsom altered his mind and went home to dinner, but on many occasions the similar missions of the little servant maid had no effect, as Mr Milsom often preferred his whiskey and water to a more substantial repast.

On the following day, I entered upon my duties as assistant at the Wilderness Road station.

Despite Mr Milsom's partiality for hot whiskey and water with lemon in it, his books were all very nicely kept; his writing was very clean, neat, and good, and as he had been without a clerk for some weeks, he evidently had been hard at work; for what with booking the passengers, making up a daily report of all tickets collected from the passengers, on which the progressive number of each ticket and the station from which it was issued was entered, booking out the goods, which included a daily collection by the railway agent of meat, butter, and poultry, for various London salesmen, taking account of all inwards goods, answering all letters of enquiry, sending in the daily, weekly, and monthly returns that were required by Mr Fretsum, the London accountant, Mr Milsom must have had more than enough to do.

I readily applied myself to the goods inwards books, which branch of railway work I had already mastered, and then Mr Milsom gave me lessons in giving out the tickets and change. How often I wished for a little of Joe War's masterly style in issuing tickets and giving change, when I felt awkward, and was obliged to make a small calculation in pencil, besides keeping the passenger waiting whilst I did it: but it soon came naturally to me, and in less than a month I found I could take a couple of hours in the afternoon for my own recreation.

The river was not far distant, and as I had my double-barrelled gun and my fishing rod with me, the moorhens and the fishing provided ample amusement for myself and Dido. This pleasure was, however, cut short by Mr Milsom receiving the following letter from Mr Peltum, the district superintendent:—

'District Superintendent's Office,
Snorum.

'To Mr Milsom,
Station Master,
Wilderness Road.

'Dear Sir,

'I am surprised to hear from Mr Sprigalilly, the Great Smash Company's Telegraph Superintendent in London,[1] that although the Company have provided you with a telegraph instrument, together with an alphabetical code, &c., neither yourself nor your staff have taken the trouble to learn how to send or how to receive telegraphic messages; and I beg now to inform you that I shall visit your station on the 1st proximo, and that unless I find that some one is proficient, I shall then report the matter to the Directors, who will probably question your adaptitude for the post of station master.

Yours, &c.,
F. J. Peltum.'

'Mr Struggles', said Mr Milsom, handing me the letter, 'you must learn the telegraph.'

I mentally abused the telegraph, because once learnt, I had heard that it must be watched. Hitherto, the wind whistling through the wires outside, and the little needle on the instrument inside, had not caused me any anxiety, but I now looked upon them as the claimants of all my future liberty.

Some correspondence took place between Mr Sprigalilly and Mr Milsom, and in three days a man arrived at Wilderness Road station with a dummy instrument to give me the first lesson.

A dummy instrument is, to all appearance, a similar one to those with which the telegraph wires are connected, only it is not a fixture, and it has a double face, and instead of the movements of the needle being caused by electricity, they are produced by the movement of a handle. The teacher sits on one side of the instrument and the pupil on the other, and in this position I again began to learn my alphabet.

I need hardly tell my readers that a boy who can give his whole mind

[1] C. E. Spagnoletti. The account given of him here is a farrago of spite. For the career of this remarkable man see E. T. Lascelles, *Proceedings of the Institution of Railway Signal Engineers*, March 1941, 70–72.

and attention to the matter will learn the telegraphic alphabet of the single needle instrument in less than half the time taken by a man, and as my mind was not overcrowded at that time, I learnt sufficient in one day to enable my teacher to compliment me upon my progress, and to tell me, that having gone so far, he would leave the dummy instrument with me for a week, at the end of which time he should commence to talk to me on the real instrument from London.

I experienced some difficulty in getting anyone to practice with me. Mr Milsom declared he would never learn or have anything to do with it. The porters were busy with their work or their ale-house amusements, and I had to fall back on Bob the signalman, who sat in his signal box many a long night without any kind of amusement but his trains.

The staff at this roadside station was composed of only seven—viz., Mr Milsom the station master, myself, Bob the signalman, a policeman who had charge of the points and signals by day, and also collected the tickets from the passengers, a goods porter, a parcels porter, and a porter who assisted generally.

The station was on the main line, and as our staff was only able to get through the work comfortably in easy times, it necessitated a great rush when there was anything particular to do, and as I was rather fond than otherwise of muscular exercise, the porters soon learnt to court my friendship for the little assistance I occasionally rendered them. They used to compliment me by talking to themselves in the following manner when they knew I could hear:—

'Our Mr Struggles is the one to load flats of meat and butter. You should just have seen him stack it up in the truck last night. Why we had done in half the time; hadn't we, "Mark?" ' (Mark was the christian name of Mark Slope, the parcels porter.)

Then Slocock, a tall porter who was the one who assisted generally, and who had been known to drink four-and-a-half gallons of beer in one day and evening without being overcome, said—

'I say, Mr Struggles, its the sheep fair to-day, and we've got orders for 20 trucks comin' down off the empty presently. Bring the little Dido down and help us load 'em, will 'e. We shan't begin afore eight to-night, and its beautiful munelight. That little dog of your'n he's better nor all them sheep dogs as comes 'ere, and if e'er a one on 'em fights w'un to-night, I'll kill un; if I don't, I'm dairnd.'

'Twenty trucks', said Jack Rawlins, the goods porter, who always declared he was christened Jack, and priding himself thereon would not be called John. 'Why it will take us half a day to get 'em across the line for loading, and we can't push two at a time unless Mr Struggles will lend us a hand.'

'I wish', said Slocock, 'that old Farmer Short had got this 'ere farm down 'ere now. Why when I fust comed 'ere he used to lend us a trace 'orse to come and pull 'em across, but this new cove what's took the farm wants to be paid, and Mr Milsom says that old Peltum won't pass it in the pay sheet, and says cos we allus done it, we must keep on doin' on't; but now, I asks, aint it different? When I fust comed 'ere, we only loaded two and three trucks, but now we've got orders for twenty to-night. Mr Struggles', continued Slocock, 'I 'opes no offence, but begging your pardon, sir, you aint stood your footin', and we should very much like to drink your 'ealth if you don't mind, sir. If you believe me, sir, I be that dry as I believe as 'alf a pint would 'iss all the way down my throat, sir, and I can't spet a sixpence.'

'Well done, Slocock', echoed the rest, and one of them gave him a hearty slap on the back, whilst he held out his hand for a shilling, which I felt bound to contribute.

'Thank'e, sir,' said Slocock, and with the utmost economy of both time and words they were all on their way to the station hotel to drink my health.

The station was thus left to me and the sparrows, which made themselves quite at home. They built in the spoutings, ate the grease that fell out of the axle boxes and hopped up and down the platforms unmolested. No one ever disturbed them. They scarcely moved out of the way of the porters, and only flew away when the passengers and the trains came in. There was something that reminded me of home in their everlasting 'chow, chow', and I occasionally brought them a few crumbs.

Bob, the signalman, was instructed to come on half a day extra on this occasion, to get ready for sheep loading. His usual day's work, or rather night's work, was from 7.0 p.m. until the down goods in the morning had passed, which was due at 7.0 a.m., but rarely went down before 9, consequently Bob averaged from fourteen to fifteen hours for his pay of 15s per week, and no overtime was allowed unless he came on half a day for special duty, in which case the 14th proportion of 15s was added to his pay. The pay, too, was always one week in arrear, as the sheet was made up on the Saturday and forwarded to Mr Peltum, who returned it after making sundry alterations—never adding, but always striking out some item—on the following Friday or Saturday.

That afternoon I had an hour's practice with Bob in his signal box. *In* his signal box I say, but half in and half out I ought to say, for there was only room for one person. In those days, there was no locking gear system, and the men could not, as now, remain by their fireside in a glass-house and turn signals and points, but they had to run, whatever the weather, to the mouth of the siding and open the points, by turning a lever on the spot. Neither was any pathway made in order that they might the better perform this duty, but the packers (who were for the most part paid by contractors who undertook to keep the line in order at so much per mile) took a delight in making the road of the roughest possible stones and ballast, which never settled down into a flat path, but crippled the signalmen, and made them all walk, like old London cab horses, off the stones.

As the safety of the trains thus depended on the vigilance of the signalmen (a risk partially obviated by the present system, which prevents a signalman from leaving his points wrong and his signals right), the Directors believed that the signal box should not be a source of comfort to the occupier. No door was provided, but the signalman was allowed to turn it round according to the direction of the wind. Bob had, however, stolen a march on the regulations, for he had grown two huge bushes of the tea plant, which met at the top, and formed a complete arch, and which, together with the signal box, a little brick paving, and a few odd pieces of rusty sheet iron interlaced in the top of the tea trees to make it watertight, formed quite a little Robinson Crusoe dwelling.

At intervals, as we rested from the tedious practice of the telegraphic alphabet on the dummy instrument, I elicited from Bob how he had built his little habitation. The roofing in the little tea tree was, he told me, composed of old tea trays and tea kettles battered out, which had come down in the truck loads of London refuse, used as manure by the farmers, and the paving was brick bats collected in a similar manner; 'and my little garden', said Bob, 'I wish I had as many sovereigns as I've buried cats and dogs in him, what have come down from London. The carters they always give them to me, because they are most too hot for them.'

Bob assured me that the first winter he was at Wilderness Road station he was 'well nigh *frozed* alive', and that the second winter, it 'warn't much better'; but his mother having given him two little tea trees, and he having got it a bit dry under foot, and built up a bit of a fireplace, kept going with coal he picked up on the line and which had shaken off the trucks when they were shunting, it was not so bad now. Bob had put a seat in his signal box, and planted primroses and violets outside.

The whole structure was one of the most comical combinations of nature and art, but there was a neatness and ingenuity that at once told you that Bob was a man who could adapt himself to circumstances and improve the opportunity with the best means at hand. The garden was part of the railway bank, and the soil was the vilest greasy clay; but what with the mixture of ashes from his fireplace and the combination of dead cats and dogs, Bob had got the ground to work so that he could grow vegetables to vie with those who had the best of gardens. His French beans were prolific, and his potatoes immense, and he could always make up a bunch of flowers, which Bob boasted were the produce of a packet of seeds some lady had thrown him from a carriage window of a passing train.

Night came, and with it the sheep loading; the approach roads were lined with flocks of sheep waiting to be loaded, and it was a mystery that the sheep did not all get mixed up, as indeed they would but for the dogs, who sat for hours between the droves in the middle of the road whilst their masters, the drovers, drank and smoked at the public houses. The neighbourhood was alive with the sheep, and their incessant cries of 'ma', 'bar', resounded the whole night long. Poor sheep, they were innocently going to the Metropolitan Market, never to return to the beautiful Downs where they had been reared and fattened.

Dido and myself made ourselves very busy, to the infinite delight of Slocock and the porters, and Mr Milsom occasionally left his whiskey and water at the hotel to come and see if we had completed our task of loading, in order that he might make out the invoices.

Mr Milsom having informed me that bread and cheese and one pint of ale was allowed by the Company to the assistants, I accompanied him to the hotel.

There was a neighbouring farmer in the bar parlour, and a glance at the old landlord sufficed to tell me that something was wrong. The disparity between the age of the landlord and his wife was, as I have before said, very great, and to make matters worse he was of a very jealous turn of mind and most sedate. Now Mrs Finch was inclined to be lively, and made free with the bar parlour customers, but on this occasion matters had gone beyond the powers of Mr Finch's endurance, and he now ordered the farmer to leave the house. This he at first refused to do, but as the landlord despatched someone in quest of the village policeman, and as this policeman was due round on his beat about this time, the farmer left. This was the first outburst of this kind that had occurred, and as the landlady's familiarity and the landlord's jealousy were at any moment likely to subject an accused party to a display of rough music,[1] I lost no time in making further enquiry for private lodgings.

[1] The knocking together of pots and pans. It was a common practice for villagers to make this din outside the house of one of their neighbours of whose matrimonial conduct they disapproved.

The dummy telegraph instrument went back, and my London instructor commenced to talk to me on the proper instrument. I was calling for him shortly after this, when my calling was interrupted by some other station, who said—

'Who are you?'

I replied as well as I could, when I received the following message:—

'Tell Milsom to look out for Calcraft; coming down by 10.30.'

I could not conceive what he meant, as I had not heard of any execution that was to take place in the neighbourhood,[1] neither could I see how Mr Milsom could be affected if there was to be one, as he was not under sentence; but as Mr Milsom had gone across to the hotel to take an early luncheon I thought I had better go and tell him, although I considered it was perhaps only a joke.

Addressing myself to Mr Milsom, I said—'I daresay, sir, some fellow is only fooling me on the instrument, but he said I was to tell you to look out for Calcraft coming down by 10.30. No doubt, I added, it is a joke.'

To my surprise this information electrified Mr Milsom, and I really began to associate it with the drop scene; his usually flushed face turned quite white, and he quiveringly replied—

'Joke be hanged. You'll live long enough to find that it is no joke. Don't you know that Calcraft is our auditor', and striding towards the private parlour, Mr Milsom said—

'Struggles, I want to speak to you.'

I followed Mr Milsom into the room, and he closed the door.

'Struggles', said he, 'I'm done!'

'Done, sir', I replied. 'What do you mean?'

'Done', repeated Mr Milsom, and he wiped the cold drops of perspiration from his forehead.

'Never say die, sir', I put in.

'Ah, Mr Struggles, you don't know. The fact is, I paid my rent this morning, never dreaming that Calcraft would come again between this and pay day, which is only three days distant, and I shall be found short in my cash, and then its all up. Here,' said he, handing me his gold watch and chain, 'I will order a cab, and you take this straight to Wilderness and pawn it. Get what you can on it, and come back like lightning; but first go to the station and bring me £1 in change to book the next train with.'

I obeyed, and tendered Mr Milsom the keys of the ticket cases and cash drawer, the latter, of course, containing the takings of the day.

---

[1] Cf. p. 20, n. 2.

'No', said Mr Milsom, 'you take the key of the cash drawer and leave me only the keys of the ticket cases, and then I can keep Calcraft at bay until you come back. Mind, I shall tell him that you are gone to get some coppers for change, so you had better bring some.'

With these instructions, I mounted the box of the cab with the driver and was about to start, when I suddenly recollected that I had £5 in gold in my box. Dismounting, I found Mr Milsom fortifying himself with a stiff glass of whiskey and water. I told him of my little reserve, which he assured me was just the amount required, and he begged me to retain his watch chain until he should return the £5. This I declined to do. The cabman was paid and dismissed, and as it wanted half-an-hour to the time of arrival of Mr Calcraft's train, Mr Milsom prevailed on me to take a glass of sherry at his expense, and I was glad to have been of service to him.

A few minutes before the appointed time, we crossed to the station. Mr Milsom placed the £5 in the safe, and as the train was signalled he went out to meet Mr Calcraft. My curiosity also led me in that direction, and I looked anxiously along the train expecting to see a tall gentleman in a frock coat alight. No one whom I could possibly associate with such a position got out of the train, and I returned to the office under the conviction that we had after all been sold.

Mr Milsom soon came in. He was talking to some little dark man who carried a small black bag, whom I mistook for a Jew pedlar; and as I was anxious to chaff him about his unnecessary alarm, I remarked aloud, 'What a sell!' Mr Milsom faced me immediately, and frowning severely held up the first finger of his right hand. I could not comprehend him.

Was it possible that the little man he was talking to was Mr Calcraft, the auditor? It could not be! But it was no other, and in a moment a recollection of his short stature, long body, with short legs, green complexion, without a pretence to whisker or moustache, distrustful eyes, flashed across my recollection as his being one of the clerks who was sitting at the head of a table in Mr Fretsom's office in London. I could not be mistaken, for he was the only person who had any pretensions to rotundity of body. I had compared his appearance with that of the other clerks at the time, and wondered at it. But now I saw at once that he fattened in the country, and adjourned to the London office occasionally only.

Mr Calcraft did not attach anything personal to my remark, but he went on talking to Mr Milsom.

'I suppose', said he, 'you did not expect to see me again quite so soon, but I heard that you had a protégé of Mr Butcher's here as booking clerk, and I was anxious to "make his acquaintance."'

Here he poked Mr Milsom in the ribs with one finger, and they both laughed until Mr Calcraft had a violent fit of coughing. When he had recovered from this attack, Mr Milsom looked at his watch, and said something about luncheon.

'Yes, yes', said Mr Calcraft, 'you know I like just a glass of ale and a crust about eleven o'clock; but don't be in a hurry, Milsom, you know me. Now,' said he, 'I'm not come to have a regular audit this time; I'm merely come on a visit.'

'On a visit?' he replied.

'Yes, on a visit; but now I'm here, there are a few old friends that I always like to shake hands with, and let us proceed. First of all, there is my old friend in prison, Mr Petty Cash; how is he? Let me shake hands with him.'

Mr Milsom unlocked the safe and produced my £5.

'Well done', said Mr Calcraft. 'Why he is looking as bright as gold'; and he laughed immensely at his own pun.

'Next, there are my old friends the train book and the cash book; I mean the daily remittance book. Let me see if they are good friends still.'

So saying, he compared the one with the other, and finding that all the takings had been duly remitted to London, including the morning's cash the receipt for which he brought with him, he declared them to be good friends still.

'Now', said he, 'let me look at my old friend, the coal sold book?'

Mr Milsom handed him the book, but explained that there was a ticket issued to one of the men for 10 cwt. of coal which had not been posted up, because he had not paid for the coal. Calcraft made a note of it.

'Now, my young friend', said Mr Calcraft, 'let me overhaul you?'

Thrusting his hands into his trousers, he surveyed me from foot to head, until I felt quite indignant at his impertinence.

'Milsom', said he, 'he is very tall, but don't you think I shall bring him to my level?' and then he laughed immensely, and coughed again.

This done, he compared my train book with the tickets, and having found the entries and cash correct told me that I might run loose until presently.

'Now, Milsom', said he, 'I will go and take luncheon with you, but my motto is "Business first and pleasure after."'

Whilst Mr Milsom was locking up and replacing the books, Mr Calcraft asked about the new people at the hotel—whether there were any fish to be caught, and if Mr Milsom had any fishing tackle. They were about to depart, when Mr Calcraft enquired as to whether I was not coming, and eventually I accompanied them. Mr Calcraft had a great deal to say, but nothing to pay; nevertheless, he gave us to understand that it was quite an honour our being allowed to treat him; he continually said he was not a proud chap, and never wished to oppress; 'but', said he, 'Business first and pleasure afterwards.'

Mr Milsom whispered to me, 'would I mind running up to his house with three bottles of stout and a pint bottle of port wine, and tell Mrs Milsom that Mr Calcraft would be up to dinner, and that she was to cook the hare that had been sent.'

Mrs Milsom did not look at all amiable about cooking the hare, which she said ought to have been down an hour ago, and that she had sent for steak; but I suppose she made up her mind to do it, for she requested me to send Slocock up to skin it.

Mr Calcraft and Mr Milsom did not confine their operations to beer and cheese, for they had cigars and sherry on my return to tell Mr Milsom the time his dinner would be ready, and after a while they came across to the station where I had been busy for some time.

'Now, Ernest', said Mr Calcraft, 'Ernest Struggles. Is that right? A good name, Ernest, shows you really are in earnest'; and again he laughed at his own wit.

'Now, Ernest, where is your parcels cash book?'

I produced the book, which had been as yet kept by Mr Milsom.

'Now, Ernest, do you know what a "paid on" means?'

I confessed that I did not. Mr Calcraft looked across at Mr Milsom, who was quietly finishing his cigar and sitting on the counter, and said—

'Do you remember, Milsom, when I taught you what a "paid on" was?'

Mr Milsom nodded, and Mr Calcraft continued—

'Very well, Mr Ernest. You see', said he, turning out both his trousers pockets, 'that these two pockets are empty. Now, Milsom', said he, 'give me two one-shilling pieces.'

Mr Milsom did so.

'Very well', continued Mr Calcraft, 'you see I put both shillings in one pocket. Now that is a "paid on," but presently I put both shillings in the other pocket. Now that is still a "paid on"; but now, in your mind's eye, write debtor over one pocket and creditor over the other, and then put one shilling in each pocket. Do you see it?'

I told him I could not quite understand it, whereupon he hammered the desk with his fist, and repeated the trick over and over again, occasionally remarking to Mr Milsom, 'they always stick at this, like the "*ponus asanorum*."' His Latin was evidently abroad. He was in the act of repeating this, when the station master's little maid came to announce—

'Please, sir, the hare's cooked.'

Mr Milsom took hold of Mr Calcraft's arm, and would have led him off, but Mr Calcraft said—

'No; I'm determined not to taste bit or drop until I have taught this young man what a "paid on" is.'

With this he repeated the whole thing, and then said—

'Now, sir, do you understand?'

I confess I prevaricated strongly, for I said 'yes', but in truth he had only mystified me.

'Now, Mr Milsom', said Mr Calcraft, 'I am ready to accompany you to eat forty hares if you like; but business first and pleasure afterwards.'

So saying, they went in search of the hare, the three bottles of stout, and one of port. I was very glad not to be of the party. Mr Milsom and Mr Calcraft did not put in an appearance again until about fifteen minutes before the last up train. There were no passengers in when they arrived; they were both exceedingly jolly, and had caught about six little perch and roach. Mr Calcraft sat on the counter, and sang 'The Maid of Llangollen.'

'Good night, Ernest', said Mr Calcraft; 'don't forget what a "paid on" is.'

I was more fortunate in my next search for lodgings, for I met Farmer Short, who said he admired my dog, and conversing with him about the probability of my obtaining lodgings, he offered to take me if his wife was agreeable. Mrs Short was agreeable. I was accordingly stowed away in their cottage, with a comfortable bedroom, and the best parlour allowed me. Wilderness Road station was not far from the river, and the station and line were occasionally enveloped in a very thick fog. On these occasions, we were allowed to employ one of the permanent-way men to stand all night on the line beyond the signals with his hand lamp, and detonating signals, to repeat signals given by the auxiliary, in order to call the attention of the engine drivers to the fixed signals. In the absence of this precaution, a fatal accident had occurred about twelve months previously. It was not, therefore, to be wondered at that Mr Peltum should have issued special instructions that whenever a fog set in a man was to be employed for that purpose. For standing all night on the railway in the manner described, the man received one day's pay, and the men could rarely agree as to whose turn it was to come on for that duty. Neither of the men referred to lived within one mile and a-half of the station, and the road to their cottages lay across a long moor, which I had traversed with dog and gun only. It was about eight o'clock one night when Bob the signalman came to Mr Milsom to say that 'the fog was a getting up, and we ought to have a man out.'

'Very tiresome', said Mr Milsom, 'but I have no one I can send for a man I cannot leave the station, and our spare porter is ill.' Turning to me, he said, 'Will you go, Mr Struggles?'

I was never afraid of a fog, so I undertook the journey, little thinking what a task I had before me. Those of my readers who have performed similar journeys can sympathize with me. It was all very well until I reached the moor. There I missed the track, which was very narrow, and not much worn. My first intimation of my mistake was a plunge into a ditch, up to my armpits in mud, and green duckweed. Cold and shivering I crept out, and was then confused as to whether I ought to go to the right or to the left. I at last determined on keeping to the right, and after carefully groping round the moor by the side of the ditch for a long time, I found myself at the entrance I had passed half-an-hour before. Again I started, and this time I was more successful, and came to a cottage. Judge my disappointment when I was informed that I must go still further. Reaching the cottage, I imagined all my trouble was at an end; but upon enquiry whether George Watts was at home, I was informed he had gone to a Temperance meeting at Wilderness, and the woman enquired—

'What's the time?'

I could not tell her the correct time, as I had no idea how long I had been wandering about the moor; my waistcoat and watch were all stuck together with mud, so I guessed at it, and told her I thought it was about nine o'clock.

'What do ye want on un?' she asked.

I thought I had better explain who I was, and I did so. Then said the woman, 'Jack Freebody's at home, for I sin un gu 'ome tight, two hours gone.'

Tight or no tight, I made up my mind to secure Jack Freebody, and after going up a lane and over a stile, according to the woman's directions, I again found myself knocking for admission.

It was a long time before I roused anybody, and I was almost despairing, when another woman, Mrs Freebody, I supposed, put her head out.

'What's up? what's up? what's up'? said she, in a breath.

I told her I wanted Jack Freebody to come on as signalman for the night; that I was wet through, and would he come with me quickly, as I had fallen into the ditch.

She communicated with Mr Freebody, whom I could hear administering the most fearful oaths on my head, and wishing I had been drowned ten times afore I'd a come there at that time to fetch him out of his bed; he hoped all the trains would run into one another, and knock the station down afore he got there.

'You'd better go; you'd better go. You'll get a day for't,' I could hear Mrs Freebody saying; and at last, oh, what a relief! the staggering permanent-way man rolled out of his cottage to go with me to Wilderness Road station to protect the lives of the public.

He was a lovely specimen of the British workman, and his smell of stale beer and tobacco added to his loveliness.

'Wait a bit', he said, and pulling out a small tin box, he asked if I would have a bit of baccy. I declined, and he put as much as would fill a pipe into his mouth, which amused him until I handed him over to Bob the signalman.

Farmer and Mrs Short were very attentive to me in my dilapidated condition, but I caught a severe cold, which almost laid me up; and indeed I think but for the kind attentions of Mrs Short on the night in question, my teeth would have chattered on until now.

They were nice homely people, who had associated with well-informed neighbours, and I soon left the best sitting-room and joined them in their family circle, which was far more comfortable to me than the bar parlour.

There was no church at Wilderness Road, but there were three villages—all provided with churches[1]—within a radius of two miles, and one of these villages boasted of a very kind and good man, the Rev. Fearnone. He often went by train, generally had something to say, and unexpectedly called on me at my lodgings one tea time.

'Mr Struggles', said the Rev. Mr Fearnone, 'I have come uninvited, but if you will permit me I will take tea with you. I am so pleased to think you have found such comfortable quarters; the Shorts are very worthy people, and I was delighted to see you at church. I do hope you will continue to come, and there is always a seat in the rectory pew for you. Do you know I am a shareholder in the railway, but I was sadly deceived as to the Sunday trains, and indeed I still hope to see them abolished; for what have we gained by expeditious travelling if we have lost the Sunday? You may depend upon it that the Sunday travelling is not a source of profit to the shareholders; it is unnecessary, a bad example, and an abomination. How can the Directors expect a man to be a God-fearing, good, conscientious man, when they rob him of his chief opportunity of improvement—viz., his Sunday. I had sad trouble with the navvies who made this line. When they first came here and I went near them, they would set their dogs at me and would not hear me, but before they left many of them attended my church; and one Sunday when I could not go to them, they actually sent to know if I was ill. I had much to be thankful for at last. Of course,

[1] Cholsey, Moulsford, and South Stoke.

you know the responsibilities of the position in life you have chosen', continued Mr Fearnone; 'they are many. There are very few positions in life where a man has more opportunities of exercising his moral authority, and above all "charity", than the position of a railway official. You are bound to meet with all classes of society, to deal with all cases of emergency, and it is constantly before you to do this or to do that. Have you ever stood on a railway platform and contemplated a whole train load of human being passengers? Oh, if you could know the secret of each human heart what a volume it would produce, and how wonderful it would seem that under such vastly different objects all were bound to travel. There is nothing more like the journey of life than a railway train. All may have different pursuits, but all are going on together towards the same end; and although some of their journeys may be shorter, there is a certain destiny for all, "the end." As you advance in position, you will have more men to command, and more opportunities of administering charity; I do not mean by alms, but by deeds. Your example will emulate and stimulate the actions of those under you. Yours will be a sacred trust, for to your care will be entrusted the lives of many thousands; but remember the rich can always command attention; it will be the poor that will need your care. You will be called upon to make great self sacrifice, as no conscientious station master can ever throw off the burden of his vocation, his mind must necessarily be always prepared to meet and to deal with any emergency, and his children—the trains—are so often out of order that they must not be left to care for themselves. Still you can be very happy if you take pleasure in your business; it will almost become your recreation. Juries may excuse railway accidents, but, to my mind, they are always traceable to the individual neglect of some person who, although not bound by any particular rule to do that particular duty, might have prevented that accident.'

Such, and a great deal more, was Mr Fearnone's reasoning, and we soon became fast friends. I returned his visit on the following Sunday, and we were getting on admirably, when matters were suddenly cut short by my removal.

Mr Peltum had written to say that he wanted a booking clerk for Puzzle Junction Station,[1] and had instructed Mr Milsom to send me there at once. He was not very amiable about it, and unburdened his mind to me in the following manner:—

'Struggles, you are to go to Puzzle Junction by Mr Peltum's orders. You will get no rise of pay, and that old Mulberry, the station master,[2] will lead

[1] Didcot.

[2] J. Peach, afterwards Divisional Superintendent, Penzance.

you a pretty time of it. He never keeps a clerk six months; never does any work himself; encourages the men to sneak of you; you will have double the work to do; and he will sneer at you morn, noon, and night. When shall you be ready?'

'Never!' I replied, 'if that is the man's character. Why can't I remain here?'

'That', said Mr Milsom, 'is a matter between Mr Peltum and yourself; but if you do not intend to go, I must inform him, only don't say I influenced you.'

Mr Peltum was written accordingly. The porters hoped I would not go to Puzzle Junction. They gave the place a dreadful character, and as to that 'Old Gooseberry', which, by the bye, was Mr Mulberry, the station master's nick name, why no name was bad enough for him.

On receipt of Mr Milsom's letter, Mr Peltum telegraphed as follows:—

'Send Struggles here first train.'

Poor Struggles knew what this meant, and as Mr Milsom agreed with me that I was to be suspended if I refused to go to Puzzle Junction, we advisedly forwarded the following reply:—

'Struggles now conforms. Shall I send him to you, or to Puzzle Junction.'

To this message Mr Peltum replied:—

'To Puzzle Junction, immediately.'

## CHAPTER IV

*Puzzle Junction—Mr 'Gooseberry'—The Station—Experience at a Junction—Lodgings over a Tap-room—Sheep—Third Class Trains—The Clerkships—The Locomotive Department*

It was only six miles to Puzzle Junction, and although I had never alighted, I had passed the station, which was between Wilderness Road and Snorum Station. I hoped I could continue my lodgings at Wilderness Road, and accordingly provided myself with simply a change. As the train which conveyed me pulled up, one of the porters called out, 'Puzzle Junction. Change here for Snip, Snap, Snorum, Borum, Bass', and I stepped out on to the middle platform at the junction. Everybody was too busy to notice me, as there were three trains in at the time, but at last I enquired of a porter as to the whereabouts of the station master?

'That's him', said he, pointing to a very tall, thin man on the opposite platform, 'but he will be on this platform if you waits a minute.'

So I waited a minute, and five minutes, during which time I could but notice my future master's extraordinary gait and appearance. Although very tall, he lost quite two inches by stooping. But for an occasional shout—such as, 'Are you right that side; now, then, get in, get in; what are you at? what are you at'?—I should not only have failed to recognize my superior officer, but I should probably have mistaken him for a tramp.

How easily we may be deceived, and how little did I then know of the abilities of the Puzzle Junction station master, who, with his aquiline hard features and straight hair, then suddenly crossed the line in front of me. When I saw he was disengaged, I stepped up to him and said—

'Mr Gooseberry, I believe?'

Oh, that fatal mistake, and what it cost me. What I would have given to have re-called it, and yet there was not so much difference between 'Mulberry' and 'Gooseberry', but I had called him by his nickname, and he knew it. He eyed me attentively for some time, and then replied—

'Mr Gooseberry, indeed! and who are you, and what do you want of Mr Gooseberry?'

I at once saw the error, and commenced to apologize.

'Oh, no', said Mr Mulberry, 'we have commenced with Gooseberry, and we will go on with Gooseberry; but mind how you gather the gooseberries. There are some thorns in the tree.'

So saying, he turned on his heels and left me standing there. I never felt more humiliated in my life. I felt sure that he knew who I was and what I wanted; I also felt satisfied that the more I attempted to correct the fatal error, the less he would be likely to believe me. I had no pass or ticket, and the collector demanding one, I told him my business.

'I cannot pass you', said the Collector, 'without Mr Mulberry's order; he has gone down into his garden, but perhaps the booking clerk knows about it.'

I jumped at the chance of seeing someone to whom I could explain my mistake. It was not long before the booking clerk and myself were talking it over, and he enjoyed the joke immensely. I did not.

It was this booking clerk that I had to succeed, but I will first describe the station itself. It was a junction, and passengers changed there, I might say, for everywhere on the Great Smash Railway. The trains from the west came there to meet trains for the north, and *vice versa.* Stopping trains shunted there for express trains to pass them; the cheap trains up and down both shunted for an hour and a half, as it was the practice in those days to run one cheap or third-class train only in each direction, and to make that train shunt and stop as often as possible, in order to make people pay second-class and express fares.

No one who travelled third class in those days was apparently entitled to a particle of respect, and the third-class carriages were little better than cattle trucks. What with the stopping, changing, and starting, Puzzle Junction was a very busy place. The station itself was like a dirty old barn, with both ends knocked out to allow the trains to run through; the roofing was blackened with smoke, and the paint all blistered. There were four roads for trains to stand under this roofing, or, strictly speaking, in the station, and five very narrow platforms.

The only communication between the platforms was by means of an underground passage, so that supposing you alighted on platform 1, and wanted to go to platform 4, you had to go down a little trap-way passage entrance, pass under Nos. 2 and 3, and come up again at No. 4.

The passage itself was simply filthy, as the leakage from the engines above, as they stood waiting, caused a continual trickling of water, which corroded on the walls in a slimy coating, sufficiently to spoil any clothes that came in contact with them. There were some directions painted on the walls below which no one appeared to understand, besides half the passengers did not know if they were going north, south, or west; thus the directions described the platforms, and as no one was below to direct the passengers, they invariably came up at the wrong entrance, and had to go back and up again until they came to the right platform, often missing their train.

There was a goods shed and an engine shed, but the work of the goods office was transacted in a room adjoining the booking office; not because it should be a source of comfort to the clerks, but in order that the two duties might be combined, to save expense.

Thus it happened that the goods clerk and the booking clerk were together; or when I say together, I should mention that a passage of about five yards long only parted the two offices, and we were able to converse aloud by raising our voices. The station itself was above the ordinary level of the road by some twenty steps, but the booking office was on the ground level, and communicated with the mouth of the underground passage before referred to. Mr Mulberry's private office was upstairs on a level with the platform, and for this I was thankful. He told the clerk, who was leaving, to initiate me as to the ticket cases, and to hand over the keys to me on the following day. The number of tickets was ten times as large as that at Wilderness Road station; the booking was of a different nature, as the people for the most past booked to Puzzle Junction and then rebooked to some other station, all coming together, and all wanting to be waited upon first.

The most unfortunate part being that the counter was an open one without any shelter for me, and not like Joe War's office at Snorum, where he could shut up his pigeon hole and tell them to *wait*. In frosty weather the ink froze on my desk.

Thus it was arranged that I took my stand as booking clerk at Puzzle Junction Station without one word of introduction with Mr Mulberry, save that I had addressed him as 'Mr Gooseberry.'

The tickets very much puzzled me.[1] Numerous as they were, they did not cover one-half of the stations on the Great Smash Railway, it being the custom to print tickets only to those stations for which there was a frequent issue. A book was provided with a blank form of ticket, and I had to fill up one of these tickets when a passenger wished to go to a station for which I had no tickets printed.

---

[1] A simple description of the ticket system in operation on the G.W. and its associated companies is given in the *Handbook Guide to Railway Situations* (1861), 14–16.

Unfortunately I did not know the names of many stations on the line. I did not know in which ticket case to search for the ticket, for there were three cases full of them, and I had nothing to refer to to see if I had tickets printed for that station. Further, in case there were no tickets printed, I had to hunt in three books to find out the fares, and was even then unsuccessful sometimes. The clerk who had charge of the goods office, the whole of which work he had to do without assistance, had never been in a ticket booking office, so he could not help me. I could not leave my tickets to ask Mr Mulberry to come and show me, and indeed I afterwards ascertained that he could not have done so, as he did not know where to find the tickets himself even if he would; so I stood at that open counter on that first morning, and I may safely say for the first week, most incompetent to fulfil the duty.

The consequence of this was repeated and gross insults from the public to myself, which fairly baffled me. Perhaps eight people were waiting for tickets whilst I was searching for a ticket for the ninth, and during my search I was repeatedly obliged to hear the following remarks, which you may rest assured were most encouraging to me:—

No. 1.—'Lively cove that; just left school.'

No. 2.—'Left school, indeed! just left his mother, you mean.'

No. 3.—'And the sooner he gets back to her, the better for the travelling public.'

No. 4.—'Just like the Great Smash Railway. Its only the same game over again.'

No. 5.—Knocking violently on the counter with his money: 'Come, come, sir! Do you mean to give us tickets or not?'

No. 6.—'If I miss my train, I shall sue the Great Smash Railway, and report you.'

No. 7.—'Here's a cove that's off. I baint a goin' to stop for no ticket;' and he goes.

No. 8.—A pale-faced woman: 'Oh, dear! oh, dear! and I have left my little ones in the train. If it should start before I get back, what would they do, the pretty dears.'

All this transpires much quicker than you have read it, but at last the tickets are handed out, the change given, and the *dreadful passengers* gone. What a relief it used to be to me, and how the perspiration used to trickle down my face, and my heart beat.

This was not the only annoyance to which I was subjected, however, because all passengers having to change from the down trains to go in another direction had to pass me; and as I was the only visible official at the entrance of this sudden bend to the tunnel foot passage, no one ever omitted to enquire of me as to which was the way they had to go to the train for this and that station. I confess I knew no more about it than they did, and being unable to tell them, I pretended not to hear.

This would not do for a set of cattle dealers, for they made a halt, and one of them reaching over the counter with his long ash stick poked me in the side. I pretended to be indignant, but they set up a laugh, and one of them shouting—

'Why, the fool don't know his self', they went on.

If they had come that way a month later, they would have found a very different man, for in that time not only had I become quite familiar with the stations, tickets, and platforms, but I could book the passengers very readily, and was quite at home and amused with the 'British public'; but I shall never forget the process of learning and the bitter sarcasm of Mr Mulberry and the travelling public.

It was the custom to take the day's receipts to the goods clerk at night. He received £70 per annum, and was therefore designated my superior officer by Mr Mulberry. He took the cash and the account of it up to Mr Mulberry. Mr Mulberry signed the account, and returned it, together with the cash, to be placed in the iron safe for the night, whence it was removed and sent to London by first train in the morning, in which train was another larger iron safe, which very much resembled a shark, for it swallowed everything and disgorged nothing, and it was too heavy to move. There was a revolving lid at the top of it, which acted like a turnstile, letting all in but none out.

Now my fellow clerk was a very peculiar man. He was a gentleman by birth and education, but he was very strange. He was my senior by six or seven years, nice looking, but very pale, slender figure, and curly black hair.

He had evidently sought refuge in an occupation on the Great Smash Railway to hide some family trouble. He would not converse; would sit for hours before the fire, holding his head in both hands brooding over his trouble, and report said he had left a wife somewhere. He simply did his work, brooded, sighed, and retired daily. It did not trouble me, as I was fully occupied without his society, but his manner was at times offensive. He expected more homage from me than I considered £10 per annum extra warranted, and at last we both took our stand upon our dignity, which led to terrible results.

Part of his allotted duty was to pay all the men at the station, and for this purpose he had provided three wooden cash bowls for gold, silver, and copper coins. One of these was missing, and he jumped to the conclusion that I had it.

'Will you turn up that cash bowl?' he said at intervals during the day, until it became quite annoying, and I at last told him I should be obliged by his not referring to it again, as I could assure him, 'on my word', that I had not seen the bowl.

'It's my impression that you have the bowl', continued Mr Hensler, the goods clerk.

This was too much for me, and in a moment I had told him that it was my impression he was no gentleman, and he had rushed upstairs to Mr Mulberry. The station master came down with Mr Hensler, his head arriving in sight before his tall body, and having beckoned me into the goods office, closed the door, and addressed me as follows:—

'Young man, Mr Hensler has been to explain to me about an altercation with reference to a cash box, and if I had been in his place, do you know what I should have done?'

I confessed I did not know, to which Mr Mulberry replied,

'Why, I should have kicked you out of this office.'

The effect of these words was like magic, for in an instant my coat was off and on the counter, and I stood before Mr Mulberry, with my fists up, challenging him to 'come on.' Whether Mr Mulberry thought I should be a difficult opponent, or whether he was afraid of compromising his position as station master by entering a combat—out of which I feel sure he would not have come without a scratch, and possibly with a black eye—I do not know; but as someone knocked at the office door at the moment, he opened the door and took advantage of the opportunity to walk away.

This was the second interview I had with Mr Mulberry. On the first occasion I had called him 'Mr Gooseberry', and on the second I had challenged to fight him. I began to reflect on my position, and for two long months I never exchanged one word with him, although we met very frequently.

Mr Hensler had told me that I should be reported to Mr Peltum, and dismissed, but Mr Mulberry did not report me, possibly because he had no right to threaten to kick me.

Thus we worked on in silence, he with his goods work and I with my bookings, and my only friend was poor old Dido. I was obliged to abandon all idea of living at Wilderness Road, and accordingly I repaired thither to remove my belongings.

Slocock, the porter, found me out, and again headed a deputation to solicit money to buy beer.

'You baint a going, sir; not promoted; and all without our a drinkin' of your 'elth, sir? Can't you leave us the little dog, sir, for busy nights?'

There was no getting out of the beer money, and whilst they were regaling themselves, I walked down to wish Bob, the signalman, 'good bye.' He was shunting some goods trucks off a down train at the time, and, to my astonishment, an excursion train dashed through the station on the same line of rails, as I was walking towards his box. When I got there, I found Bob on his knees. He was praying.

'Oh, Mr Struggles', said Bob, 'did you see that excursion train go through, and will you go and look at my signals to see as they are against her?'

I looked, and the signals were certainly at danger, showing a red light to an approaching train. The train had dashed through the station as Bob was shunting, and by a miracle one-half the train being shunted was in the siding, and the other half was clear of the main line, scarcely a yard.

'It will sure to be a Board job', said Bob, 'but I don't mind, so long as nobody is killed. Another instant, Mr Struggles, and nothing on earth would have saved them!'

The other train was just backing. Mr Milsom was sent for, and a full report was made to Mr Peltum. Two days later Inspector Bull[1] came to Puzzle Junction to question me relative to what I knew of the occurrence.

Inspector Bull might be described in two words, for he was Peltum's bully. He was a tall, stout man, of about forty years of age. Originally, he was a policeman, but he had been promoted to be Mr Peltum's confidential inspector and assistant, and in that capacity he watched the actions of all, sneaked of anybody, pounced on the men by night and by day, got up evidence, and in fact did all the dirty work for Mr Peltum.

When he had taken notes of what I had to say, Inspector Bull told me that he had no doubt Mr Peltum would require me to attend before the Board of Directors on the following Wednesday, as the driver of the excursion train declared that the signals were all right for him to pass Wilderness Road station, whereas Bob, the signalman, declared they were standing at danger.

A pass was forwarded to Mr Mulberry, and on my way to London, Bob, the signalman, joined me.

'Ah, Mr Struggles', said Bob, 'we all thinks our troubles is the worst, but there's a worser job happened this morning. Poor Mr Milsom is found dead in his bed.'

I was very much distressed to hear it, and on enquiry, it transpired that

---

[1] Inspector Noble.

he was superintending the loading of some sheep the night previous, and that one of them, in trying to escape, had bunted him in the stomach, which knocked him over. He only complained of slight pain, and went to bed in his usual spirits. In the morning his wife heard a gurgling sound, and before she could get assistance, he was dead. His wife was left penniless.

When we arrived at the London station, we were marched up to the very passage outside the Board Room where I had been on the day of my appointment, and our case, being an important one, was the first called on. The engine driver, the stoker, Bob, and myself were all called in and the Locomotive Superintendent, Mr Gabriel Gouge,[1] was in attendance to support his own men. So great was his interest, and so doggedly did the driver and his mate lie, that I am convinced that had it not been for my humble testimony, Bob, the signalman, would have been dismissed the service. As it was, the Directors could not well dispose of the fact of my having seen the signals against the train; but one of them, an elderly gentleman, with grey moustache, whiskers, and very little hair on his head, who I afterwards found out was called 'The Captain',[2] cross-questioned me severely as follows:

'Where were you when the train ran through the station?'

'Where was the signalman when you got to him?'

'How long have you been in the service?'

'How do you know whether the signals were at danger or not?'

Failing thus to shake my testimony, Lord Farrington, the chairman of the directors,[3] was about to decide against the driver, when Mr Gabriel Gouge reminded him that the driver would not be likely thus to sacrifice his life. After all, it was a drawn battle; we were all sent back without any decision, and the fortunate passengers in the excursion train were happily none the wiser.

I had hitherto been lodging at the hotel opposite Puzzle Junction Station, called 'The Junction Hotel', but as that was too expensive a matter for £60 per annum, I determined again to seek private lodgings.

Since my challenge to fight Mr Mulberry, Mr Hensler had treated me with some respect, and having enquired of him as to lodgings, he told me that it was simply impossible to find any, for Puzzle was only a little village, and the engine drivers, porters, and guards had already monopolized every

---

1 (Sir) Daniel Gooch. He was Locomotive Superintendent of the G.W.R. 1837–64, and Chairman 1865–89.

2 Capt. Bulkeley of Windsor.

3 Lord Barrington was Chairman for only a short time in 1856–57, though Vice-Chairman 1843–56 and 1857–63.

house in the place. If, however, I liked to board with him, probably I could get a bedroom somewhere, and it would be more comfortable for two to board together, as we could live better. My search for a sleeping room was in vain, and I was about to give it up when, as a last resource, I thought I would enquire at a little public-house called 'The Owl and Moon.' They knew of nothing, but had a room they could themselves let to me for 3s 6d per week if I liked to take it. I did not like the idea of sleeping at such a place, but as the landlord and his family were smart people who had been groom and servant in some gentleman's family, and as the room looked very clean, I took it. My bedroom was immediately over the taproom, and to the ceiling of the taproom was fixed what the men called a 'spinning jenny', which was a revolving hand, like that on a clock, with a number of figures round it. It was with this that the customers won and lost pots of beer, and in turning this, they had broken away the ceiling, so that I could distinctly hear all that was said below as I was in bed. The first night I had the pleasure of hearing myself talked about by some of the porters—who had come to spend the evening—in the following terms:—

'Got the young un up here a sleeping from the station? He's a fiery young blood. Did you hear of his taking his coat off to "Old Gooseberry?" Made the old man set his back up more nur ever; but he didn't dare put claw on the young un.'

'I likes un for sticking up to "Old Gooseberry",' said another voice, 'but if he don't look out, "Old Gooseberry" will pay him in his sneaking way when he aint aware on't.'

'Ah', said a third, 'if he set that "Tenfield" on to him, I'll be bound he'll run him down.'

(Tenfield was the parcels porter, who was encouraged to sneak to Mr Mulberry of everything that transpired about the station.) There were as many as twelve guards living at Puzzle, and perhaps six who were paid there resided elsewhere. Amongst the latter was a guard named Barfleet, who assumed the airs of a 'swell', and was almost patronizing in his attentions to me. I naturally took a dislike to this man, and although at first I was glad for him to come and take any tickets he required for passengers upstairs, who preferred paying the guard to coming along that dreadful underground passage themselves, I soon had my suspicions that he occasionally took two tickets and paid for one only, for I could not make my money right.

I repeatedly requested this guard to keep outside of my office; he as often disregarded my request, until one day I actually caught him in the act of taking two tickets when he had only paid for one, and I taxed him with it.

He was very indignant, insulting, and said it was a mistake, and he refused to go out of the office until I apologized. My apology was of that nature that he had a black eye for nearly a fortnight afterwards, but it had the effect of keeping him in his proper place for the future; and I believe, when asked about his eye, he attributed it to the slamming of a carriage door.

My readers will, no doubt, come to the conclusion that I was a pugnacious young man, but I beg to say that, although naturally of a very hasty temper, I was not fond of fighting; but it so happened that these two encounters did take place, and as I have no wish to represent myself as a model of innocence, I must relate them.

My new lodgings saw very little of me, for the monthly abstracts were about, and they were the first I had ever made out. All the numbers of tickets had to be entered on a large sheet, and compared with the numbers of the previous month. As the numbers were all progressive, it was thus ascertained how many tickets were missing. These tickets did not all belong to the Great Smash Company, as we often booked passengers beyond their line, and in all cases a separate abstract or account had to be made out for each company.

In those days I invariably made out ten large abstract sheets, and in fact did the work of division, which is now done by the Railway Clearing House, in some cases dividing one ticket into five proportions, according to the mileage of each company. I could not well commence until night, and I should like to have received some instruction. It would have saved me many hours, but I preferred doing it over and over until I got it right to asking Mr Mulberry. The first month's balance was a sad one for me, for I had sold four tickets for £1 each less than I should have done, owing to a mistake in a figure made in the labelling by my predecessor. There was no remedy for me but to pay the amount, so I made a special entry in the train book, and thereby forfeited my first month's pay, save a few shillings, at Puzzle Junction Station. It was anything but encouraging for me to hear the porters carousing at night on the 'tips' they had received, when I felt that I had worked for nothing.

The abstracts over, I had a little time again on my hands, and a few brisk walks, with my gun and Dido, braced me up again. Whilst I was thus trespassing, I came upon a field not far from the station where there were some rabbits, the tenant of which field was a cattle dealer whom I knew, and in this field were twenty neglected sheep attacked with the fly. One poor thing was dying, and half eaten; two more were almost hopelessly attacked, and not one in the flock was free. Anything more inhuman cannot be pictured, and you may be sure that I lost no time in communicating with the owner. I was obliged to ask Mr Mulberry for an extension of time to enable me to go to the cattle dealer's house, and when he granted it, he remarked that he wished he could 'tie him behind the next train' for so neglecting his sheep. Of course, I expected the cattle dealer's people would be much obliged to me for pointing such a thing out to them, but I was disappointed. Mr Webber, the dealer, was not at home, and his son, a youth of about eighteen years of age, was indoors, and invited me in. The youth's reply to my statement was—

'Oh, its only them cull sheep.[1] The best of them only cost 20s a head, and we always expects to lose some that way. It don't pay to keep shepherds. Father will be at home to-morrow night, and I will tell him.'

Amongst other things of which I was possessed was a cattle medicine chest, which I had purchased during my farming days, and in this I had a lump of camphor, which I had often used for dressing sheep. It was a filthy, tiresome job, and it took Dido and myself some hours daily to destroy the maggots. The one first struck was dead, but beyond that I saved the flock. Dido used to sit and keep them all up in a corner whilst I caught them.

Despite my having done this one act of charity unobserved, as I thought, it came to the ears of Mr Webber, who made it his business to thrash his son with a ground ash stick, and to offer me any recompense I might wish. This recompense I declined to state, but I craved permission to sometimes take a walk with Dido and my gun over his farm. This permission was readily granted, and I was installed with a shooting manor. *Hurrah!* I was vain enough to think Mr Mulberry envied me when he saw me come home with the linings of my old velvet shooting jacket hanging rather baggy, but I never omitted to send Mr Webber half what I shot.

Mr Mulberry commenced to converse with me, and calling me up, he communicated some very disagreeable news to me.

'Mr Hensler has to take charge of a small station', said Mr Mulberry, 'and until Mr Peltum sends another clerk, you must do his work.'

This, indeed, was bad news. No shooting, very little time for meals, and on duty from 6.50 a.m. until 11 p.m. No help for it, however, so I put my gun on one side, and tried to keep pace with the work.

At night I had to take up the cash to Mr Mulberry, and thinking this a favourable opportunity to get some information from him about booking out the goods that were going out that night, I addressed him as follows:—

*Self*—'There are the goods to book out to-night, sir.'

*Mr M.*—'Well?'

---

[1] Inferior sheep, not fit for breeding.

*Self*—'I have never booked any goods out, sir.'

*Mr M.*—'Quite time you learnt to do so, then. What did you do in the goods office at Snorum?'

*Self*—'Inwards goods, sir.'

*Mr M.*—'Then, what on earth can be the difference? In one case you receive an invoice, check the rate, calculate the charge, and enter it in a book; whereas in the other case, you take the consignment note, fix the rate, calculate the charge, and make out the invoice, copying that also. Don't trouble me with such nonsense.'

*Self*—'But, sir, I have the ticket booking to do, and I do not know at what rate to charge the things.'

*Mr M.*—'Then, sir, refer to the Clearing House Classification, and if the invoices are not properly made out, I shall report the case to Mr Peltum.'

Now if Mr Mulberry had said, 'Struggles, it is so long since I made out an invoice myself that I have forgotten all about it; I don't want to expose my ignorance to you, therefore I bully', he would have told the truth. It took me all that night to find out how, and to invoice those goods. The reference to the Railway House Classification was not quite so easy as one would imagine.

Goods of apparently the same quality were separately classed according to the use to which they were put, and there did not appear to me anything which would serve as a criterion as to the heading under which the respective articles were placed.

When the clock struck 4 a.m., I had finished, and Mr Mulberry had probably passed the greater portion of his night's rest.

If any of my readers should be railway men, let me here remark that there is no danger of their easily forgetting what they have had to find for themselves. I can speak from experience.

For three long months I did the double duty of Puzzle Junction Station, and in my capacity I was frequently dancing attendance on Mr Mulberry.

He did not come on duty until 10.30 a.m., at which time the down express came in. When this train had gone, he opened what letters there were, and placed them in various pigeon holes in his office, for others to hand in reports to enable him to reply to them; but the largest of these unfortunate pigeon holes was my own, and in this one he placed all letters that had reference to the accounts, to parcels, to tickets, to goods, to telegraph, and all other matters of minor importance which did not come from Mr Peltum, the divisional superintendent, or someone of importance. This system did not leave much for Mr Mulberry to do, as he had merely to affix his signature to my replies in most cases, and so he usually took himself off to his garden or to his luncheon at the hotel opposite until the one o'clock express, after the departure of which he went to dinner until 4 p.m. The trains were rather thick about this time, and Mr Mulberry usually walked from platform to platform to see if he could catch porter or passenger in any way transgressing. He had a special antipathy to engine drivers, guards, and commercial travellers, and bitterly I have heard them all curse him. Smoking was one of his great providers for occasions for attack; but I will presently tell you of one instance in which his over-zealous conduct brought the Great Smash Company to grief.

At six o'clock, Mr Mulberry retired to tea, and at 9 p.m. he returned to his office, where he invaribly sat until midnight. Why he selected these three hours for work was always a mystery to me.

Before Mr Mulberry took his seat at 9 p.m., he opened his office door and and called out lustily, 'West'. Now West was the foreman porter of that station by night. His duty was to superintend the shunting of all trucks, the unloading and reloading of all 'station truck' (as they called a truck containing goods for several stations) goods, to keep the men in order, start the trains, and account for all delays. He was in fact night station master, only he was dressed in the Company's cord clothes, and his pay as night foreman was only £1 per week. He had never been on duty a day in his life; that was his boast, and he had been at Puzzle Junction ever since it opened. West was a very clever man, and but for two failings he would at the time I am writing this have been in a good position in the railway world.

His first failing was his being scarcely able to read or write, and his second was an enormous appetite for beer and tobacco.

It was reported that he lived almost entirely on beer and chewing tobacco, and that he spent quite 20s per week in those articles. His wife did a good deal of washing, carried on a kind of box and cox bed letting, and sometimes when West had some overtime, he gave her a trifle from his weekly sum.

When Mr Mulberry called out 'West,' you might fairly wait a few seconds to allow West time to take a huge quid of tobacco from his mouth, after which he would reply, in a voice even louder than Mr Mulberry's, 'Yes, sir.' West then joined Mr Mulberry in his office, the door closed, and everyone felt that everybody was safe for at least an hour, Mr Mulberry being occupied.

The porters, guards, and police took advantage of this hour by sending for beer in the porter's room, a filthy hovel, where they sat and polished the table and seats with their offensive corduroy clothes.

I never intruded on their privacy, but I knew from the conversations that took place in the public-house where I slept, that this room was strongly associated with the taproom of the same. The room was a specimen of the carrying out of the old adage, 'What's everybody's duty is nobody's duty', and thus it was very rarely even swept out; beyond which some of the guards who worked fish trains used to provide a supply for our men, the cooking and storing of which gave the room an extra flavour.

One poor switchman suffered death as the penalty of one of these diversions, for he neglected, until too late, to return to his post to turn his signals and points, and in the darkness and excitement of the moment, he walked on the wrong line, was knocked down, and literally cut in two pieces.

His wretched remains, the inquest, and the funeral are things not easily forgotten, and the switchmen of the present day may be thankful that, by the new system, their lives are so much less endangered.

As no clerk had been sent for the goods office, and bearing in mind that the salary was £70 per annum, whereas I was only receiving £60, and not one penny extra for doing the double duty, I applied to Mr Mulberry for the higher appointment, and requested that a second clerk might be supplied.

'You are just too late', said Mr Mulberry. 'I have a letter from Mr Peltum to say that a Mr Badger, brother to Mr Badger the assistant secretary,[1] is coming to do the goods work.'

As this would be a relief to me, I was glad; but imagine my surprise at finding that Mr Badger was only newly appointed in the service, and positively knew nothing of railway work, having just come from behind a draper's counter.

As this gentleman figures very largely in my railway career later on, I must trouble you with a description of him. He was a draper's assistant all over; not in the least like his brother. He was not more than 5ft. 7in. in height, thin, a prominent nose, no whisker, and a young moustache. He wore a frock coat, most extravagant check trousers, with an immense silk tie tied in a bow, and I could tell at a glance that he brought with him an empty skull, and the full weight of his brother's influence and position.

His assistance was no relief to me at all. Mr Mulberry would have nothing to say to him, and when I remonstrated, he simply replied—

'You had better be careful, Mr Struggles. If Mr Peltum was made aware of your remarks, I don't think they would assist you in your railway career.'

Mr Badger would not take his Sunday on duty. He was scarcely civil, and never thankful to me for teaching him his duty, and when it came to

---

[1] The second Badger was A. Higgins, later Superintendent, London South-West Division.

the time for making up the second month's abstracts, he expected me to do his abstracts for him as before, and wrote to his brother on my refusing to do so. Mr Badger's brother wrote to Mr Mulberry, and as Mr Mulberry stormed at me and refused to listen to reason, I enclosed him the following letter:—

'Puzzle Junction Station.

'Dear Sir,

'In consequence of the injustice of your having appointed Mr Badger, who is unable to do his own work, over my head at a salary of £10 in advance of my own, I respectfully beg to give you one month's notice of my intention to leave the Great Smash Company. I have an offer of an appointment under the head brewer of one of the London Brewery Companies, to which I can proceed at once if you will release me.

'I beg to remain,

'Your obedient Servant,

ERNEST STRUGGLES.

'To Mr Mulberry,
'Great Smash Railway,
'Puzzle Junction.'

This letter was forwarded to Mr Peltum, who made it his business to come to Puzzle Junction at once, and I was sent for to Mr Mulberry's office.

'Mr Stwuggles', said Mr Peltum, 'I am suppwised to wern fwom Mr Mulbewwy that you are gwilty of insubowdination. Now insubowdination, Mr Stwuggles, is a thing I never can countenance, and unless you go on with your work at once, I shall suspend you.'

Mr Mulberry then silenced me, opened his office door, and showed me out. I tried to argue the point, but to no purpose, and I should certainly have carried out my intention of leaving, but for the fact that Mr Badger was appointed as station master at a little station, and that I was appointed chief clerk at £70.

A new booking clerk was sent to follow in my steps, and all this was done in the brief space of one week. This booking clerk was a nice fellow. He had been clerk in a brewery, and he had been at Wilderness Road since I left. He knew something of the work, and we got on excellently. He was rather hasty, and I suppose from that fact arose the nickname I gave him, which was 'Phiz', for I used to tell him he went off like a bottle of ginger beer, which was quite harmless after the cork had been out a minute.

Although I say it, the work of Puzzle Junction was never done so well as then, for we used to help one another, and then Phiz would come and beat up the rabbits and moorhens for me and Dido. Phiz was no shot, but he liked beating. He, too, got very much attached to Dido, and Dido was dancing attendance on us all day. If I wanted change for a sovereign, I used to wrap it in paper; Dido would take it to Phiz, scratch his leg with his paw, and wait for the change. Phiz also taught him to go over to the hotel, with a penny in his mouth, and buy himself a bun, which he always brought back to the office to eat. If I wanted to go out, Phiz would book my goods out; and if he wanted to go anywhere, I booked his trains. Thus we defied 'Old Gooseberry', and made ourselves as comfortable as we could.

It was at this station that we played rather a laughable trick on an old farmer who had been up the country, and who, returning home by the cheap train, had left his umbrella at Jam Junction Station.[1]

The cheap train, as I have before told you, had to shunt a very considerable time at Puzzle Junction, and the guard, 'Old Morris', was in the habit of going out of the station to direct the passengers to the Public, where he used to drink with most of them.

There are statistics of the number of threepenny-worths he used to drink, but at last he became artful, had a little water as a substitute for gin, and divided the surplus with the landlady.

Old Morris used to call out, 'Puzzle Junction. We have an hour and a half to wait here. Any lady or gentleman requiring a cup of tea or any other refreshment will be kind enough to come with me, and I will show them the way.'

He never failed to have twelve and sometimes twenty followers, others joining afterwards, and the porters used to say, 'There goes "Old Morris" and his lambs.'

Phiz would go up with me to meet this train, and one morning we espied a very large green umbrella in Morris's van.

'Here's a "Mrs Gamp",' said Phiz. 'Where did you get it, Morris?'

Morris said he found it at Jam Junction, and that he thought it belonged to the old farmer just then getting out of the train.

'Take it down to the booking office', said I; 'we will have a lark with Farmer John.'

I am sorry to tell you we were rather fond of a little fun. 'Mrs Gamp' was carried off in triumph, and when Farmer John applied to the 'guerd', as he called him, he was referred to me, and I took Farmer John to the office to see what I could make of him.

The umbrella was, of course, placed out of sight, and Phiz pretended

---

[1] Reading.

to be very busy writing when we arrived. I pretended also to treat Phiz as my superior officer, and told him that *this gentleman* had lost something.

'State your case, sir', said Phiz, whereupon Farmer John took off his hat and proceeded as follows:—

'Well, doant you zee, zur, I be a varmer, I be, what lives down below, and I've bin up the country, zur, to a vair. We 'ad to w'it an hour, zur, at that there Treacle Junction.'

'Treacle Junction', interrupted Phiz. 'I suppose you mean Jam Junction?'

'Ah, that bin it, zur, but in course it's all the zame to I. H'wever, I 'ad to get another ticut there, and as I couldn't get nowhere nigh'st the winder where they gives 'em out with my umbrella, I puts un down, and bless me if I didn't come awi wi'out un, and I be that vexed I can't tell'e. 'Taint the vallie on un, but e's bin in the vamily so long. There, to tell 'e the truth, zur, 'taint mine, 'tis my mother's, and she zays to I, she zays, the last words a comin' awi she zays, "John doant 'e go fur to lose my umbrella", and if you thought, zur, as I could get un, bless me if I would'nt zooner lose a day nur go 'ome wi'out un, zur, if you think no one aint a took un if I goes back, zur.'

'No necessity for that, my good man', said Phiz, 'we can telegraph and ask them about it.'

Farmer John laughed outright.

'I've 'eard of this 'ere taligraph', said he, 'but I believes it's all a dead take in; but thaire now, zur, if you can get my umbrella down by un, to jump all they posts, and come along on them wires avore my train starts, then I beliv' in the taligraph, and not avore.'

'Well, my good man', said Phiz, 'you go over to the hotel and have your luncheon, and I will see what I can do if you will be back in a quarter of an hour.'

'I'll go, zur, and I'll come back; but doant you think, zur, as I beliv's ye, cos I knows you be only making a vool of I', and so saying he went.

When he had left we determined to hang the umbrella on the telegraph wires and take him to it, and accordingly a ladder was procured and the umbrella suspended.

True to the time, Farmer John returned, and said, 'Well, genemun, where's this 'ere umbrella?'

Phiz took up the ruler, and rattling it against the iron ticket stamp on the counter, he pretended to converse by telegraph with the people at Jam Junction. Putting his ear to the ticket stamp, he asked Farmer John if it was a green umbrella with a buck's horn handle, and a patch on the top?

Farmer John replied 'That's 'e', with evident glee.

To which Phiz added, 'Coming down! coming down!'

'Well, I'm blessed; well, I be blessed'! said Farmer John, and at Phiz's request we walked up the steps and down the line to the place where we had suspended the umbrella.

The farmer gazed with mouth open, and when the umbrella was obtained and handed to him, he examined it, opened it, and having satisfied himself that it was his own, he exclaimed, 'Well, if I hadn't zin it I'd a never 'ave belived it; but zeein's belivin.'

We might have added, 'Not always, my friend'! but we did not undeceive him, for fear his village should be deprived of an everlasting fact.

Farmer John was very anxious that we should go and take a 'zup of zumon' with him, but we were quite satisfied with our sup of fun.

Mr Mulberry had been acquainted with our joke by Tenfield, the parcels porter, and that night he accosted me as follows—

'If you clerks are so fond of playing practical jokes, I will find you scope for your energies in such a manner that it will benefit your employers. I should think you were well set to work this morning; very creditable, indeed. Now here is a case that you will be kind enough to take in hand, and unless you succeed I shall bring the matter of this morning under the notice of Mr Peltum.'

Mr Mulberry then read aloud a letter from London, respecting hampers or baskets of fruit, to the effect that not a single consignment had been forwarded from Puzzle Junction for some weeks past but some of the apples had been abstracted, and giving an opinion that the pilfering took place at our station.

'There', said Mr Mulberry, 'before you play any more practical jokes, just find our who steals these apples.'

'But how are we to discover it?' I asked.

'That', said Mr Mulberry, 'is your look-out. Of course, if you stand by the fruit undisguised it is not very likely you will catch anybody. Use your own discretion.'

Phiz and I decided that it was a very disagreeable job, but seeing no other way of getting out of a scrape, we decided to attempt the detective.

Most of my readers have doubtless seen a tall tree or shrub packed in a basket and tied round with straw, and it was thus that we determined to stand secreted by the apples to catch the thief. I borrowed a basket and some straw, and got a branch of fir tree to stick in the top. Phiz and I tossed to see who should be packed, and it came to his lot. At the given time I packed Phiz as a fir tree, bound him round with straw, addressed him to 'Mr Smith, 25, Exchange Street, London, *with great care*', and had him carted to the Goods Station about the time that the apples arrived. Not even the man who carted him knew any difference, but Phiz said they nearly upset him taking him out of the cart, and he was frightened to death for fear they should stick a knife or prong into him through the straw. He remained about two hours packed, during which time I found an excuse to go to the goods platform twice to see how he held out.

Phiz was terribly cramped, and had almost determined to give it up and come out, when one of the night porters came into the shed, and, pretending to light his pipe, turned the gas out. He then commenced to grope about, and actually thrust his hand through the straw and caught hold of Phiz's back. He could not have had the slightest idea as to what he had touched, for muttering 'what in the world is that?' he went on examining other parcels until he came to the apples. Phiz could not see him, but he imagined what he was doing, and, accordingly, when he was about to leave, Phiz came out and detained him.

He had about a gallon of apples in a bag, and although he begged very hard first, and then tried to wrestle away, Phiz stuck to him and brought him up to Mr Mulberry, who was certainly delighted, and but for the porter's absconding, he would have punished him with the utmost severity of the law. He actually grew quite polite to me, and a day or two later sent for me to know if I would shoot two pigeons that escaped from a basket, which was booked by train as a parcel. They were beautiful pigeons of the pouter tribe, and whether they were accidentally or purposely released by the porters I cannot say, but they needed no string to secure them when they started again on their journey. They had alighted on the Junction Hotel roofing, and in company with Mr Mulberry and, I may say, the greater part of the station staff, I made for the two pretty pigeons with my old double muzzle loading gun in hand.

'Shoot them as they are', said Mr Mulberry; 'they are close together.'

'No sir', I replied; 'I am no pot hunter.'

Mr Mulberry must have forgotten himself, for he actually said, 'If you put them up, I'll bet you half-a-crown you don't kill them both.'

'Done, sir', I replied, and in a brace of shakes I had put them up and brought them bouncing down, as good a double shot as ever I made.

The men gave me quite a cheer, Mr Mulberry handed over the half-crown, and took the pigeons to repack them.

As he took them he remarked, 'Two dear pigeons, and not able to cook them; I rather wish I had forwarded the basket without them; but, there, the shot was worth something'; and I hear that he talks about it to this day.

We spent Mr Mulberry's half-crown; but what must have been the surprise of the people who expected pigeons alive to receive two dead ones; and how difficult it would be for them to account for the shot marks, seeing that the basket was not injured.

Mr Mulberry and I got on better. He actually asked me to go with him to his garden. I gave him several useful hints, and some very substantial help with the spade and fork, which were tools quite familiar to me.

One part of Mr Mulberry's duty was, I soon found out, most objectionable to him, and that part was the enquiries he had repeatedly to make of the Locomotive Department—for he had openly defied the Locomotive Superintendent, Mr Gabriel Gouge; repeatedly reported the engine drivers for petty negligences, and thereby brought himself into contempt with the whole body. Mr Mulberry therefore handed over all matters of enquiry of this kind to me, and I had to visit the engine shed at all hours to see the men, to obtain the necessary information.

Of all men in the employ of railway companies there is not a class with which the public are so little acquainted, and yet in the coaching days the driver was the man whose society was most sought. Is it not again astonishing, that whereas the driver of a coach and four horses, value a few hundreds, and say twenty passengers, should have been a man, for the most part, from the middle class, the driver of a railway engine and train, with say one hundred passengers and so many thousands worth of property, should be from the lower orders? And, as an old coach driver once said, 'When an accident happened to a coach, *there you were;* but if an accident happened to a railway train, *where are you?*'

It would have astonished anyone to have seen, as I did, the material from which engine drivers sprung, but I will endeavour to show the class of men who were promoted to be engine drivers on the Great Smash Railway.

To begin with:—A lad seeking to drive an engine had to commence work as a night cleaner of engines. If he got on pretty well, he had others under him in time; and a very great promotion was to be 'lighter up', in which capacity he had the responsibility of putting fire into an engine four hours before she was wanted. The next step was that of fireman to a goods driver, in which capacity he had to fag for the driver and keep the fire up. If there was nothing to prevent it, he got appointed to be driver to a shunting engine in time, which is an engine nearly always kept about a station at work, and only occasionally sent away with a train. He was afterwards appointed, when a vacancy occurred, to be driver to a goods train, then to a stopping passenger train, and lastly, indeed you might almost seriously pun on the word 'lastly', to an express passenger train.

The pay of a junior engine driver (or night cleaner) at the time I am writing about, viz., 1860, ranged from 10s to 14s per week, for which he had to come on about 7 p.m., and rub the bright parts of the engines during the night with oily waste. As to education, I won't venture to make a remark about it, as the pay and the occupation altogether abolished the idea; but I will go so far as to say that some of those engaged were too dissolute and too lazy for the farmers to employ them, and although some of these might or might not be engine drivers at the present time, still they *were* there. I never attended the cleaning shed without both hearing and seeing scenes that impressed me most unfavourably. Mr Gabriel Gouge may uphold his men, but I say it was and is a great pity that he and others did not draft into the lucrative occupation of engine drivers a better class of men, who, despite the extra trouble they might be to manage, as an intelligent race of men would be able to calculate the immense responsibility of their trust, unmeasured with their own lives and a consumption of malt liquors.

It is simply marvellous that with such a training we have at the present day such an immense number of worthy men as engine drivers. Very few better class men in 1860 would have undergone the ordeal of such a laborious acquaintance with an engine as two years of night cleaning, and there was no other (neither is there now) open to them; and whilst an educated man writes as a clerk at 20s per week, an engine driver rides by him, with no social pretensions, at double the money, and enjoys his occupation.

But I have not explained their secret of success. It is this:—No sooner do they become firemen than they jump from obscurity to publicity. Not a movement at a station is unobserved; not a mile is run without the Guards timing it; not a signal must be disregarded, and they are in one straight groove from which there is no escape.

I cannot take an abstract of the cleaners who do not attain to the post of engine drivers. I cannot say that the pay they receive is adequate to the risk and danger they encounter, but I may be allowed to remark that it has always been a marvellous thing to me that such sound, good, obliging, worthy assistants should have risen to be the custodians of the public with such fearful odds against them. Nevertheless, during my railway career I never recollect receiving an unkind word or act from an engine driver, and I contend that they are marvels of manufacture. If they know nothing whatever of the nature of steam, they know a great deal about the parts of the engine, and they will pack a broken down old engine and keep her going, with a most deserving patience; whereas a scientific, educated man would not risk his life on the old blunderbus.

Still I cannot help saying that there are men living as engine drivers whose minds are not even yet sufficiently educated to enable them to realize the responsibility of the position they occupy, and at whose door lie the deaths of many passengers, although they have themselves marvellously escaped the death others suffered, and which was the result of their careless indifference.

Will you for one moment imagine yourself driving an express passenger train at the rate of one mile a minute, with Her Majesty's Ministers and four Railway Directors inside? What would be your feelings? Would you not peer anxiously for every signal, and would you not breathe freely when you saw the Prime Minister and his company alight?

On one occasion when some of Her Majesty's Ministers and four Directors were in the train, I accompanied the driver.

I had been to the station from which his train started, and being anxious to return speedily, I jumped on the engine as it was leaving the station.

'Hulloa, Mr Struggles', said the driver, 'Be you a goin' down?'

I replied that I was, and he said, 'In course you knows of that new order out, as we aint to take nobody on the engine now? but, there, I don't mind you, Mr Struggles, only you mornt let them see ye get off when we stops.'

'Let who see me?' I asked.

'Oh, we've got the big uns inside, the minstrels they calls 'em, and the Directors. The Queen's minstrels.'

'You mean Her Majesty's Ministers', I said.

'Yes, that's them; but there—there's only one of 'em as ever I knows—that's that Dizzy—cos of his curls; I could swear to he on a sugar paper, I do believe.'[1]

By this time we were travelling at full speed.

The driver then took out a thumb bit, and offering me a dirty old tin can, said, 'Drink, Mr Struggles; it's only tea.'

'How she do rock, Jim', he added to his mate.

'Steady, Jim; they've got the caution signal up yonder, but we mustn't stop if we can help it.'

The signal was taken off, when the driver called out, 'Right, Jim, let 'em 'ave it'; and he put full steam on, rubbed his nose on his coat sleeve, and continued— 'Wonder what them Directors is a goin' down for, Mr Struggles. I did hear as one of 'em was a going to be knighted; but, anyway, they will be ready for their luncheon after that shaking. I had pertickeler orders not to lose a minute, so I don't care what they ses. The old Captain is among 'em, I see, but, there, he never meddles with us drivers. Mr

[1] Disraeli's curls were the sport of all contemporary caricature. This episode must belong to a later period: Disraeli was a Minister in 1866–68.

Struggles, there's one thing I wants of you, and that's just *a drop of oil.* They 'lowances us out, and if you can spare us just a can full, if ever I gets some to spare and you wants it, you can have it again. Thank'e sir', and then he shouted out, 'Sand her!'

Jim lets out some sand, which drops beneath the wheels to make them bite the rails; the train pulls up, and I get off the wrong side to avoid observation.

## CHAPTER V

*A New Post—A Magisterial Charge—Grain Road Station—A Railway Accident—Lord Farrington—Snip Station—Death of Dido—Government Inspection—Working Single Line—A Narrow Escape—Porters' 'Tips'.*

But now, to return to Mr Mulberry and Mr Peltum. There are new things in store for me. Mr Mulberry has sent for me to his office. Mr Peltum is there, and it is explained to me that an alteration is contemplated. An Inspector for the platforms is coming to Puzzle Junction, and in consideration of this I am to be the appointed Relieving Station Master for the whole of Mr Peltum's district, to go anywhere and everywhere whenever a Station Master is unwell, or has a holiday. I am to be allowed 7s per day for expenses when I am out all night, and 3s 6d when I am out all day only, and I am to go to-morrow to Grain Road Station;[1] and all this on the special recommendation of Mr Mulberry, who is to have the benefit of my services when disengaged, and to whom I am still to look for orders.

This was quite a change for me. Phiz did not like the idea at all, as he would have double duty to do, but we determined to spend the evening together at 'Redbourne Feast', which was to take place at a village about three miles off.[2] We bribed Tenfield, the porter, to book a train or so, and risked the rest. I hunted out two smock frocks for the occasion, and two pairs of leather gaiters, which was the attire my father insisted on my wearing when I left school to learn farming; and with the aid of two cheap Dudley hats[3] and a burnt cork, we made a very pretty pair for the country feast.

Amongst the special attractions at the feast there was on exhibition a very fat woman who put her knee out of a window, which was represented to us outside as her arm, to deceive us as to her proportions, but we declined the honour of feeling her flesh to see that it was real. There was a man seven feet high, and a dwarf; a waxwork show; a sheep with five legs and

[1] Challow, formerly Faringdon Road.

[2] Redbourne must be Hagbourne, where there was a village feast on the second Tuesday after Trinity.

[3] Broad-brimmed slouch hats.

two tails; some performing dogs; and various stalls with stale gingerbread and hog puddings. But our attention was soon turned to a dancing booth, where we got on very well until two yokels claimed our partners, and as they were half tipsy and very insolent, we were obliged to leave to prevent unpleasantness, as there was a policeman engaged for the occasion. Phiz wanted to fight them, but I managed to get him away.

We were surprised to hear on our return, that there had been a dreadful row at the station during our absence, and that Mr Mulberry had locked a gentleman up for smoking and annoying the Rev. Mr Sleekplot,[1] who was the clergyman at the village where we had been feasting. The gentleman was taken before the Magistrates at Wilderness on the following morning, and this is the evidence that was offered against him.

The Rev. Mr Sleekplot attended, and said to the Magistrates:—

'I was a passenger by the fast up train from Bass Station[2] yesterday. The prisoner got into the same first class carriage. No sooner had the train started than he commenced to smoke a cigar. I protested, but he continued, and I had fully made up my mind to give him into custody at Borum Station, only just as the train was stopping there he threw away his cigar and apologized. When the train started again he lit another, and smoked until we arrived at Snorum Station. At that Station I endeavoured to explain the case, but the train started, and the prisoner was then handed over by myself to Mr Mulberry, who is present.'

Mr Mulberry then gave his version of the affair, which was very much the same, as it merely repeated the Rev. Mr Sleekplot's statement.

The prisoner, a well dressed man, was then asked what he had to say in answer to the charge? when he replied that the offence took place in the county of Lostshire, whereas he was now charged in the county of Brakeshire.[3]

'Gentlemen', said he, 'I am a Solicitor; I was specially engaged in a case which I shall now miss, and I shall sue the company for detaining me. I respectfully hold that you in this county have no jurisdiction over what occurred in another county.'

He was released, and he did sue the company, and got £80 damages.

Whilst this was going on I was in charge of Grain Road Station. It was the nearest station to a country town, three miles distant,[4] but the inhabitants

---

[1] The Rev. Richard Meredith, Vicar of Hagbourne 1825–68.

[2] Birmingham.

[3] Lostshire = Oxfordshire; Brakeshire = Berkshire.

[4] Wantage. Simmons's account of Faringdon Road station is broadly confirmed in A. Gibbons and E. C. Davey, *Wantage Past and Present* (1901), 95–96.

of that town had strongly opposed the making of the railway, and therefore there was not a large amount of good feeling between the company and the townspeople. The only accommodation in 1861 was a goods shed, at one end of which was a tiny hutch called an office, where tickets and books were kept. No platform was erected for the passengers to get into the trains, and no shed but the goods shed for them to wait in. One train per day called there on the down line, and one on the up line. I went down daily by the one, the train waited whilst I gave the people tickets who were waiting, and I returned by the train with the passengers I had booked at night. The daily receipts for tickets were from 30s to £2. The station master had one man to help him, mind signals, and do all the work of the station, and he was a dreadful writer and scholar. He could not find a house nearer than two miles to live in, and there was not a vestige of a habitation within sight. He was a very respectable old man, but he had made a kind of gipsy camp of his office. He had not been away for a holiday before, and was in fearful trouble at leaving for a few days to see the Exhibition.[1] He was delighted when I offered to cast up his books for him, several pages of which had not been totalled, 'for', said he, 'castin' aint my fort, and if you knew the trouble you will save me, you would know how glad I be for you to do it.'

After he had left, the first thing I did was to open the window of his office to let in a little fresh air, and this brought in the assistant, who declared that his master would go mad if he knew that window was open.

I determined to have a clear out, which quite frightened the man, and as he declined to 'have any hand in it', I had therefore to do it myself. The drawers contained a variety of articles; into one he had apparently combed his hair for some time, and there were the brush, comb, and hair. In another was a dirty knife, fork, and sundry pieces of cheese rind; in another, tobacco, and a strong smell of gin; and in another, onions. I swept the office out, replaced the things, and made it quite smart, but I was unable then to take advantage of my labour, as not only was it fearfully hot and the onions too strong for me to sit there, but an arrival of wasps was terrific.

I soon discovered that the visit of wasps was due to the presence of a sugar cask which was in the shed, and as it was uncertain when it would be sent for, I was at a loss to know how and where to spend the many tedious hours that intervened between the trains. Fortune, however, favoured me, for an old farmer who owned a large field of wheat in which

---

[1] The second International Exhibition in London, of 1862. Note that the date has now changed from the '1861' given above.

the station actually stood, rode up and said, 'Young man, if you sees them rooks on they thair shocks, I wish you'd holler at them!'

I offered to bring my gun down the next day, which offer was gladly accepted. It did not take me long to build myself a small summer house with the wheat shocks, and after I had put the absent station master's books straight and helped the porter do anything he could not accomplish alone, I found that a most comfortable retreat, free from wasps and the smell of onions. Two rooks suffered death as the penalty for disturbing me, and this was the first station of which I ever took charge, with two trains a day, and a wheat shock house.

A letter from Mr Peltum directed my steps, not to Puzzle Junction, but to Rock Station, to assist Mr Badger with his accounts. Never were any accounts so mystified as these, and Badger was positively civil to me at first, and glad of my assistance. It took me a fortnight to put him straight, and I was inclined to think he was grateful, when he spoilt all.

'Mr Struggles', said Mr Badger, 'when *are* you going to finish those goods abstracts? I have a letter from Mr Peltum complaining about the expense of sending you here, and unless you finish to-night I must tell Mr Peltum you are not up to such work!'

Here was a pretty thing for this upstart to say. He had so muddled his accounts that I had worked very hard to get them straight, and just as he felt himself out of his difficulties he could afford thus to insult me. I replied as follows—

'You had better write and tell Mr Peltum that you are an ungrateful snob, who, but for your brother's interest, would still be behind a draper's counter. I have been in the Company's services two years and am not yet appointed as station master—whereas you, who have not yet been three months in the service, are appointed as station master at £80 per annum, and I am only in receipt of £70.'

At this moment I noticed the telegraphic instrument calling, and as Mr Badger was unable to read it, I proceeded to take off the following message:—

'*From* Mr Peltum, 'Snorum Station.'

'*To* Struggles, 'Rock Station.'

'Mr Mulberry is laid up. Go to Puzzle Junction by first train, and take charge.'

This message ended our controversy. I took notes of the totals of his books, and packing up the abstracts to complete them at Puzzle Junction, I wished Mr Badger 'good night.' He did not answer my farewell salutation, and I believe he always secretly hated me for having spoken the truth to him.

Could it be possible that I, who twelve months before had arrived at Puzzle Junction station perfectly ignorant of anything connected with its management, should in so short a time be in the position of Station Master? Yes; there I was in supreme command, so I snatched every opportunity to read up the rule book which I had partly studied under the wheat shock at Grain Road.

Mr Mulberry was dangerously ill with gastric fever, and would be absent for some weeks. If ever there was a busy young man, I think it was myself. Not a train came into the station but I met it; not a train went out but I started it; not a letter was despatched but I signed it; not a movement escaped my notice; I stirred up some of the porters who were inclined to be indolent; I visited the lonely switchmen in their distant huts; I superintended the shunting; and finally I nearly lost one foot for life, for, whilst crossing from one platform to the other across the buffers of coaches of a train, some additional coaches and the engine came suddenly up just as I had moved my foot, and caught part of my boot between the buffer spring and the socket. However, it taught me a lesson, and made me more careful.

A very sharp letter from Mr O'Reilly, the traffic superintendent, set me to work to answer a quantity of train reports which had accumulated during Mr Mulberry's sickening for the fever. This was the mysterious work which he was in the habit of doing at night with West, the night foreman; and I could not get on without the assistance of West, who was not accessible until after 8 p.m., when he came on duty. Some of these train reports were three weeks old, and were of this nature—

'The 10.15 Up Express Goods 2 hours late in London; reports she was detained 1 hour at Puzzle Junction. What was she doing, and how do you explain delay?'

It was remarkable how West carried all these irregularities in his head, and how he could enable me to reply to them. He could even remember the numbers of the trucks concerned, and what was in them, despite the quantity of beer and tobacco consumed.

Poor Mr Mulberry gradually recovered from his illness, and sent me a note of enquiry about his garden ground at the station, which Phiz and myself had put straight for him, and for which he was very grateful. After all we discovered that Mr Mulberry had some latent good qualities which did not appear on the surface; but I never knew any man represent himself so unfairly.

He came back at last, and as the Prince of Wales was about to be married and I had an invitation to London to witness the decorations and illuminations,[1] I applied for leave of absence for that day and night, which was granted. I was charmed with the idea of a little holiday, and was in the act of packing a little bag with a change of clothes when I was stopped by a letter from Mr Peltum, who commanded me to go at once to Rock station to relieve Mr Badger. You imagine with what feelings I took charge of that station, and saw Mr Badger depart to enjoy the holiday that was fairly mine.

I was moodily pining over my lot at Rock station when Mr Hanney, the Delivery Agent, who lived at the town of Rock, came to me and said—

'Are you not going with us in the omnibus to Rock, Mr Struggles? There is room on the box seat. I can offer you a bed at my hotel, and there are to be great rejoicings at Rock to-night.'

I was not in a mood to go to any rejoicings. I had missed my anticipated treat, and without even time to write and advise my friends that I could not join them; but I could see no consolation in stopping at that miserable roadside station public-house until morning, so I reluctantly consented to join Mr Hanney.

It was a nice drive, and as my companion was full of chat I began to think I had better make the best of a bad job, and join in the rejoicings at Rock; but then came the question—How could I join; I did not know one living soul in the place, and there would be great difficulty in participating in enjoyment without friends?

'We have a Tradesman's Ball at the Town Hall', said Mr Hanney; 'I am one of the Stewards, and I supply the supper; if you will accept a ticket, I shall be most happy to present you with one.'

It was very kind of him, but could I go to a ball and not know a soul there? It was true I was in a measure prepared, for I had brought with me the things I had intended taking to London, but how could I go as a perfect stranger?

'My good sir, I am going myself', said Mr Hanney, 'and I know everybody. You can go with me.'

Thus it was arranged, and thus it was carried out so far as the starting was concerned, but no sooner had we set foot in the ball-room than a waiter rushed for Mr Hanney, and pulling him violently exclaimed—

'Oh, please sir, come directly. We can't stop the gin, and it's all running away.'

My conductor disappeared like lightning. I hoped he would not be long, and therefore waited patiently, but whether he could not stop the gin

[1] He was married on 10 March 1863.

running away, or whether the smell had overcome him, or whether he was saturated with it and had not a second dress coat (which latter was really the case), I did not know, but I stood there at the entrance to the ball room, without knowing one person there. It was not a comfortable position for so young a man, but I employed my time in surveying the goodly company. All were well dressed, and many of the girls were very nice looking. My friend did not return from his gin, so it was a case of retreat or go forward for me, and as I rather longed for a dance, I selected the very ugliest old wall flower for a partner, and popped the old question—

'May I have the pleasure of the next dance with you?'

She jumped at the chance. Probably she had not danced before, and with the exception of one little polka to which I treated her as a reward for her starting me in business for the evening, I observed she did not dance again. She seemed very pleased and pranced up wonderfully, coughed a good deal, and presently introduced me, at my request, to rather a better class individual. Step by step I got up by this manoeuvring, until I danced with my future partner for life. This young lady was the daughter of the Postmaster, and we very soon discovered that although we had never met before, we had often conversed on business by means of the telegraph. One thing is certain—if I entered that ball room without a friend, I left it with one who has never deserted me.

Now, as this is not a love tale, you must excuse my recording the little stupidities in connection with our courtship, and how I stole time to attend to the matter, but one novel feature about it was this—that we conducted it almost entirely by telegraph, and we established an alphabet of our own for that purpose, with which I shall be very happy to supply any of my readers should they contemplate a similar courtship. You must not for a moment imagine that we preferred this *modus operandi*, but you must not forget that we were both tied to our professions, and that it was a matter of necessity. Necessity is said to have been the mother of invention.

Mr Badger returned, and I went to Puzzle Junction. It was quite a gala day at Puzzle Junction, for the new room for refreshments was to be opened that day. There had been a smart encounter between the newly built hotel and the old hotel, but Mrs Jones of the old hotel, who had kept Mr Mulberry supplied with jelly and soup during his illness, had beaten Mr McGregor of the new hotel, who was a penurious Scotchman, and who was never known to give anything away but a pinch of snuff. So Mrs Jones, who had two marriageable daughters was duly installed as lessee of the refreshment room at £200 per annum, whereas the two McGregor girls were doomed to disappointment. The two families never spoke of one another, from that date, except in disrespect, which was everlastingly sealed by old McGregor dying and leaving widow and daughters *versus* widow and daughters.

It was a mystery to me how Mrs Jones could pay £200 per annum as rent, and something heavy as rates and taxes, for so small a room; but she did, and has since retired. It was, however, no mystery to the 'British Public', for everything was assessed at double the price charged at public-houses—a cup of tea was sixpence; stale buns, twopence; two pennyworth of spirits, sixpence; and, oh, if they only looked at the sandwiches, such a charge. The people who needed refreshments walked in and enquired the price, and came out again. It was only those who were fat and well clothed who indulged in them. Many a poor child had his hand squeezed and was dragged past the buns; and the pretty boxes of cream chocolate were not within the reach of those who most admired them. A glass of water was a penny. They sold cigars, although no one was allowed to smoke, and the young ladies were so nicely dressed, and their curls shone again. It is true there was a printed tariff drawn up by the Great Smash Company and framed, which was hung up behind the door out of sight, on which it said that a passenger might have bread and sausage for sixpence, also that you might have four pennyworth of gin; but somehow the sausages never came, and if anyone who happened to know of this order complained that he had been charged sixpence for gin, it was, 'But sir, you should have asked for four pennyworth; I gave you sixpennyworth.' To this the passenger invariably replied, 'that he could scarcely taste what he had received for sixpence, and he wondered what four pennyworth would have been!'

I failed to see that the 'British Public' were any better off for the room, but Mrs Jones was, and the amount collected of her for rent paid the salary of Mr Mulberry and the booking clerk. Moreover, it amused some of the young swells to get out and chaff the Misses Jones, for which they bought something, and not a day passed but somebody who had taken a little drop too much, treated the guards and porters, and it all made good for trade.

During Mr Mulberry's illness the trains had run very regularly, and Mr Peltum had complimented me on the subject, although, in reality, I had little to do with their running, any more than the prompt despatching of them; but no sooner had Mr Mulberry returned than all sorts of irregularities occurred. One of these was two goods trains trying to form the letter T. That is to say, whilst one train was passing a junction another one ran into the middle of it. The drivers and stokers escaped with their lives, but two of them were dreadfully injured by jumping from their engine, and when the driver who jumped was well enough, he gave me the following account of the accident.

'We was going down with empty coal wagons, and when we come to the junction for to turn off Snorum way—in course I shet off steam a bit for to slacken round, but the signals was right, and the sixty wagons come along beautiful. I seed as the signals was all right for we, at the tother end of the loop line like, and I puts steam on again, and I never know'd nothink was wrong till I see'd tother train, all cattle, a comin' round the corner. I opens my brake whistle, but twarnt no good. We was right bang a top on her, and I shouts out to my mate, "Jump" I ses, and I never know'd nothink more about it till I come to, on this bed, sir.'

After our friend had jumped, his engine dashed into a train load of cattle, and a fearful slaughter was the result. The ruins were heaped on the top of poor oxen and cows, six of whose misery I terminated with my old gun, but it was a sickly sight. A little white calf had been pitched out by the shock, and, falling into a ploughed field, did not appear to be hurt. The poor little thing licked the blood on its dead mother, and bunted and caressed her, almost as much as to say, 'Get up, mother, and give me some milk', and it cried after her for two days whilst we took care of it at the station.

No less than twenty-two head of cattle were killed in that accident, and it took twelve hours to get the line clear.

Of course it was nobody's fault. The signalman swore most positively that his signals were against the approaching cattle train, and the driver swore most emphatically that they were all right for him to come on.

How many trains had previously crossed each others' paths under similar circumstances will never be known.

Inspector Bull looked up a lot of evidence. The accident was reported in the newspapers, and Lord Farrington went to London especially to enquire into it.

I did not know Lord Farrington, the Chairman of the Directors, Mr Mulberry did. One of my duties when at Puzzle Junction was to take the fare book to the platforms in readiness to excess the passengers, by which meant—that in case any of them travelled in a superior class of carriage to that for which they had taken a ticket; if they came by an express train with an ordinary ticket; or if they came beyond the station for which they had taken a ticket—I had to tell the ticket collectors at a glance how much to collect, and I was also prepared to give change. It was rather irksome standing about with but little to do, and although it was no part of my duty to collect the tickets, still I preferred assisting with the work.

In this capacity I came across Lord Farrington and a carriage full of friends, chiefly ladies.

Not knowing his lordship, I asked him for his ticket, to which he replied very gruffly, 'All right.' This would not do for me, as I knew that a person having no ticket should have a pass, and that the Directors themselves have small ivory passes which they usually keep on their key-rings.

'It is not all right, Sir', I replied; 'Have you no ticket? where did you come from?'

'All right', repeated his lordship, 'I don't need a ticket.'

'Then probably you have a pass, Sir! will you allow me to see it?'

'Don't you know me', roared his lordship.

I replied that, 'I had not the honour of his acquaintance, I simply wanted ticket, pass, or payment.'

'Then go and ask the guard who I am', said Lord Farrington, 'and mind how you make my acquaintance.'

At that moment Mr Mulberry passed the carriage, and seeing with whom I was conversing, called me away.

My next outing was to Snip, which was a little road-side station. The station master there resided in a very small one-storied house, with four rooms. The house was a converted stable, but it was very comfortable, and he very kindly offered me his quarters. His housekeeper was a respectable looking person of about thirty years of age, and this lodging saved me a long lonely walk.

Never had I before seen books so nicely kept, and everything was in such nice order at the station. The waiting rooms clean, the platforms swept, and the porters civil and obliging. Everybody was friendly with the station master, and the enquiries were very numerous as to his absence.

It was quite a country place, and the traffic and people in accordance. Amongst my customers were three country girls, who called each other Sarah, Jane, and Mary Ann. The train was coming in by which Mary Ann was going to her situation as domestic servant.

They were late arriving at the station, carrying a large box. 'Hark!' Sarah exclaims, 'Jane, you gu and get the box labuld, I'll gu and get the ticut, and Mary Ann you gu and get in.'

Sarah gets the ticket, Jane gets the box labelled, and Mary Ann gets in. Sarah and Jane meet at the door of the booking office and nearly knock noses together. Jane exclaims, 'Sarah, where's our Mary Ann?'

They both rush up and down the train in quest of her until at last Jane espies her seated in the first compartment next to the tender. The engine is blowing off a good deal of steam, which causes Jane to put up her elbow as if to keep it off, and she exclaims:

'Look! Sarah! Here's our Mary Ann bin and got in next to the copper!'

This was the class of traffic at Snip Station, and I rather enjoyed the jokes until an old country woman, with a coal scuttle bonnet, entirely took me down, which she did as follows.

She had come to the station to see her daughter off to service, and, as I stood behind her whilst she was talking to her daughter, already seated in the train, I overheard the following maternal counsel, which was only answered by sobs and nods from her daughter:—

'Good bye, my dear. 'Ave ye got yer tickut all right? And yer money tied in yer 'ankerchief? Mind and 'rite. Good bye, and God bless 'e. Sit with yer back to the engin'. Look arter yer box. Let's know how yer gets there. Give my love to Martha. Be a good gal.'

I started the train. The old lady put her handkerchief to her eyes, and I still stood close behind her. The train had actually moved on a hundred yards or so when she exclaimed, 'God bless 'e,' and removed her handkerchief from her eyes. There was no one near us, and I was wicked enough to say to the old lady, 'Do you mean me, ma'am?' when she replied most indignantly, 'Don't know yer, but I s'pose yer be like Calcraft, pretty used to such scenes! It's a pity yer aint got nothink better to do nur to make fun of poor folks' troubles, but there's no knowing what y'll come to you some day', and so saying she walked off, and I felt that I had justly merited her rebuke.

My first night at Snip Station was very comfortable, but I regret to relate that the second night my friend's housekeeper had taken too much, and at 9.0 p.m. she was all but tipsy. If there is anything more disgusting than another, I think it is a drunken woman, and to be in a house with one is anything but pleasant. If she would have retired for the night I should have been very thankful, but she insisted on sitting up and making pastry. If my friend Phiz had been with me we might have enjoyed the joke, but to see a woman in her best clothes rolling flour and lard about until she was covered with flour was not a lasting amusement for a sole observer. At length, when far beyond the hour of midnight, she fell back into a chair with the dough in her lap. I put the lights out and left 'my lady' to put herself straight in the morning.

A letter from my friend Phiz grieved me sadly. It ran as follows:

'Puzzle Junction.

'My dear Struggles,

I regret to inform you of a most distressing accident to poor Dido.

You know that there are two down lines on which the down express can run through the station, only one of them is the platform line and is generally full of horse boxes. Well, to-day, the switchman had left the points wrong, and we were all dreadfully frightened by the down express running through the wrong line, when we heard poor Dido shriek out. I went to him directly and found that one of his fore feet was completely smashed. He could never have recovered, and we held a consultation and all agreed that we could not do a greater act of charity than to drown the poor dog, and which we have done. I confess I cried, Struggles. Poor old fellow, I only yesterday won half-a-crown by his retrieving a hen's egg half-a-mile, and the night you went away I took him down the line and he put up a covey of partridges which flew into the telegraph wires, he hunted round and found a brace of beauties which had knocked themselves down against the wires, and I was keeping them as a surprise for you on your return. We were all very thankful that there were no horse boxes in the line as there generally were, and although the poor dog is dead, his death is nothing compared with the dreadful accident which would have happened only for the line being clear. Mr Mulberry has suspended the switchman, but for whose carelessness poor Dido would have been spared to us. I have laid him in the sack room next to your office.

'Yours faithfully,

PHIZ.'

This was a cold morning for me, I had lost my most faithful friend, and it was many a long day before I took up a gun with any pleasure. We buried poor old Dido in a box on a mound opposite the station, and everyone was sorry; many of the porters followed.

I had to beg hard for the switchman, who would otherwise have been dismissed the service, and although he at first said, 'If it had not been for that infernal dog I should not have got into trouble', he afterwards planted a tree to mark the spot where he was buried, and thanked me for the interest I had taken in his case. It was the custom in those days to dismiss anyone from the service for the slightest fault, but I could not see that it was a desirable practice, inasmuch as a new man, perfectly ignorant of his work, was invariably placed in his stead.

Our new Inspector for Puzzle Junction arrived and was duly installed. He was a man about forty years of age. Had served twenty years in the Life Guards, and report said he had been servant to 'The Captain' who formerly had a commission in the same regiment. He still padded his chest, brushed his buttons, cleaned and polished his own boots, secured a flower for his button hole, and he paraded the platforms.

He knew very little of railway work, but was most exemplary in his obedience to his superior officers, and most domineering to his subordinates.

If Mr Mulberry had said, 'Inspector Badthings, Go and shunt the next six trains down the embankment, and cut the telegraph wires', he would have done it. But stop—in that case he might have asked for a written order. His position was very peculiar, and so far as I could see, his services were valueless, for he was not scholar sufficient to write a letter and to assist with any accounts, and he was too 'old a soldier' to do any work. Therefore he became merely a parading bully to look up the men, as a carter boy looks up his horses with a whip, and, as I have worked several stations very successfully without the aid of an Inspector, I am inclined to think that porters and others do their work with a much more willing hand if you can impress them favourably with their responsibility, without an overlooker of this kind, who often descends to pocketing their little tips, and of whose absence they always take advantage, losing moral caste directly a man of this description, himself no better than they are, is placed over them.[1]

You must not understand that I condemn Inspectors personally, as some of them conduct their sleek occupations very kindly, and are really admired by the public, who imagine them to be people of responsibility because they open carriage doors, call a porter, and say 'right' to the guard. Besides, we have at least some gentlemen for Inspectors, for instance, the Government Inspectors, who are gentlemen of good birth and education, and who were just appointed to their posts at the time of which I am writing.[2] What a satisfaction it must be to the public when an accident *has* happened to know that 'a real gentleman', appointed by the Government, goes down to the spot, taking luncheon in a saloon carriage on his way thither, accompanied by the officials of the line on which the accident has happened, and whose very frown or hint beforehand, accompanied by their presence, will undoubtedly have the effect of 'the whole truth and nothing but the truth' being laid before the enquiring Colonel or Captain Inspector, and that he will report so that no more accidents of a like nature

---

[1] Simmons's criticism here may well be justified. The duties of the station inspector did in large measure duplicate those of the station master. 'To the station inspector is confided the starting of trains', says the *Handbook Guide to Railway Situations* (13). 'He has also to act as superintendent during the temporary absence of the latter, and to see to the proper performance of the duties of the porters and policemen who may be serving under him.'

[2] A muddled statement. There had been Inspectors of Railways under the Board of Trade for twenty years past—since 1840. Of those serving at this time, only one was 'just appointed': Col. F. H. Rich, who took up his post in 1861.

may occur, or in other words, that he will actually sit in a station master's office and have the men in one at a time, and ask them to state what they know about it, and that he will write it down.

How likely it is that after Inspector Bull has been to the men and tutored them as to what they ought to say, and pointed out that if they say 'so and so' it must end in their dismissal, that they will convict themselves and the company. Pooh! don't believe it.

If Government enquiries are to save the lives of the public, I contend they should be made by practical men *before* the accidents happen, and not afterwards. Railway accidents are of such a varied nature that the fact that a Government Inspector has thoroughly investigated and reported on a case of a train running off the line this week, will not prevent one running up the wrong line next week, and the only good that I at present recognize is, that those employed to make enquiries as to accidents that *have* happened, are by this time getting some experience which they are employing for the benefit of new lines of railway, which cannot be opened without their sanction. Still I expect to live to see practical railway men as government policemen to watch the working, and time the crossing, forming, and loading of all trains on all lines, to *prevent* these accidents. Railway directors know that at the present time extra men and extra precautions are required, but taking the whole system they can calculate to a sixpence the cost of those extra precautions. They can also calculate the number of deaths that arise annually for the want of those precautions, and the balance is so much against the public that you must die on until further orders.

At present Government inspection reminds me of an incident that once occurred at Jam Junction station. The station master was an old gentleman who had been appointed by the interest of a Director, and who was not born a railway man. It was midnight, and an accident happened. The night foreman came rushing to the station master's house, which was over the station, and knocking with a pole at his window he at last attracted the attention of the station master who appeared at the window in his nightcap.

'What is it' ? said the station master.

*Foreman Porter.*—'If you please, sir, there's an accident.'

*Station Master.*—'What sort of a night is it ?'

*Foreman Porter.*—'It's dreadful dark, sir, and it rains cats and dogs, and most fit to blow the signals down.'

*Station Master.*—'What has happened ?'

*Foreman Porter.*—'Please, sir, the up goods has run off the line down below the junction. She fouls both lines, and there's two trains a standing behind her as can't come on, and the down mail is due.'

*Station Master.*—'That's a bad job. Have you ever had anything happen like it before?'

*Foreman Porter.*—'Yes, sir. Last year the down goods runned off about the same place, only she didn't block both lines then, sir.'

*Station Master.*—'What did you do then?'

*Foreman Porter.*—'Please, sir, we sent men out to stop the trains. We telegraphed to London for the breakdown gang and the portable crane. We called up all the men, and we worked single line all night.'

*Station Master.*—'Then do the same again, and mind you let me have a full report in the morning'; and so saying he turned into bed and slept soundly until morning.

But I must return to Mr Mulberry, who was not a man of this description. On the contrary, he was never satisfied unless he took the lead at a break down, and he prided himself on his superior knowledge in all cases of emergency.

It was Mr Mulberry who taught me to work 'single line', and, like Joe War, who showed me 'how to book passengers in style', a pretty lesson I had. I will relate it.

The night in question was black, and the time midnight. A train had run off the line half way between Puzzle Junction and Wilderness Road on the down line, and it had been necessary, in consequence, to work all trains, both up and down trains on the up line. For this purpose and in order that no train should meet another, I was appointed pilotman. That is to say, no train could start from Wilderness Road or from Puzzle Junction unless I was there, and if I started two trains I went on the engine of the second train to Wilderness Road to bring a down train back. I had been riding up and down for some hours, and Mr Mulberry had been superintending the clearing of the line. At last all was clear on the down line and a telegram was sent to the station master at Wilderness Road to that effect.

'We will go up the down line', said Mr Mulberry, 'and re-open it.'

'Better go up the up line as before', said the driver, 'and come down the down line back.'

'Nonsense, man', said Mr Mulberry, 'Do you think I don't know what I am doing?'

'Very well', said the driver.

'Come on, Struggles', said Mr Mulberry, and we got on the engine and started up the down line. We were tender first, with nothing to break the force of the cold, bleak current of air which our pace created, and it was hard work to keep our footing and to hold our hats on, we went at such a rate.

'How plain that light shows', I said as we rounded a corner about half-way to Wilderness.

'Bad luck!' exclaimed the driver, 'it's a train a comin'. There's no help for us. Brake her!'

He shut off steam, opened his brake whistle, and reversed his engine. We clung to the brake like maniacs, but oh, those moments. They were life or death to us. The other train saw our light, and we pulled up ten yards only from each other. We were saved. We all shook hands, and it was some minutes before we summoned up strength to do anything. Mr Mulberry's face was a ghastly picture. Had not the other driver been on the look-out, our lives must have been all lost, and you would have been spared the trouble of reading this.

It was very unfortunate for Mr Mulberry, whose salary was to have been raised, and the directors, although they thought the Wilderness station master was in a measure to blame, still they considered Mr Mulberry's venture was unnecessary, and condemned him accordingly—cutting off his expected rise of salary.

I was obliged to repeat what the driver had said, which exonerated him, and of course I was only a subordinate of Mr Mulberry's, and bound to obey him, and that was how he taught me to work single line.

I shall never forget the lesson. If any man's heart was ever in his mouth, mine was on that black night. My feelings were indescribable.

For a whole year after this I remained at Puzzle Junction nominally, but was in reality going about to relieve the various station masters. This occupation was a very nice one, because, not only was it good to have a change, but I received 7s per day expenses.

Many little incidents occurred much of the same character as those I have related to you. I overheard a great deal of the porters' conversation in the taproom with which 'Old Gooseberry', myself, and Inspector Badthings were associated.

One porter would say to another, 'I say, Bill, how did you get on with that old parson this morning?'

'Oh, "Bad Egg",' the other would say—which meant that the parson did not tip. He would then continue, 'I say, Bill, there's nobody gives so much trouble as them old ladies and them parsons. The old ladies do fork out a "bob" sometimes, but them parsons aint worth their salt. However I nipped the label off one old cove's luggage to-day. He kept me messing about for a quarter of an hour, and then said he hadn't got no coppers. When he finds his luggage he will be lucky.'

Mr Mulberry sent for me one evening to take charge of a very pretty girl. She was about 17 years of age, very nicely dressed, and she had a gold watch and chain, rings, earrings, and a gold brooch. She was tipsy. It appeared from her enquiries that she had been placed under the care of her uncle, who was going to London, and that at Puzzle Junction she had to change trains for Bass Station. Her uncle and herself had come a very long way and he had persuaded her to take some gin, which had overcome her. Poor girl, perhaps she had never had any gin before!

It was rather a delicate matter to take charge of a young lady in this condition, but I got her some tea, and kept the porters and guards from making fun of her, whilst she continually exclaimed, 'Where's uncle?'

She was very sick at last, and I got a maid servant from the Junction Hotel to come and take her over there for the night. She had plenty of money to pay for her accommodation, and looked very much ashamed of herself in the morning.

I think 'Uncle' ought to have been ashamed of himself too.

# CHAPTER VI

*Importance of Station Master's Position—An Exciseman Outdone—Nerve of a Spinster—Summoned by the Police—A Promotion with a £10 Increase*

AT last the fatal moment arrived, and Mr Peltum sent for me to take charge of a country station for good. Although Mr Peltum argued that it was for my good, I objected to the appointment, as not only did he refuse to increase salary, but I could no longer go out relieving, and thereby lost a little source of increase of income.

Mr Peltum readily divined my motive and replied, 'Very well, Mr Stwuggles, if you will stand in your own wight you must; but you won't go out weweaving [he meant relieving] any more.' Fairly beaten, I accepted the appointment.

Phiz succeeded me, and I was duly installed as station master to Hinehoe Station.[1]

It was a pretty clean little station, and, although my predecessor was removed on account of his inability to keep the accounts straight, they were a mere trifle to me after the accounts at Puzzle Junction.

The station was close to a village, but there was a town also,[2] about 2½ miles distant, for which this was the station.

With all due respect to the station masters of the present day, I beg to say that a station master at a small station was then a personage of much greater importance in the estimation of the public than he is now. It was a new thing, and the clerks and station masters were for the most part supplied from the middle class of society, and able to hold their own in a gentlemanly way; whereas, at the present day, they are, for the most part, the descendants of the porters and policemen, who, having been educated at the British and Free Schools, have been drafted into the Telegraph Office, and thence to the clerks' appointments. There is nothing sharpens the wit of a lad like a telegraph office, but it cannot be expected that the

[1] Aynho.
[2] Deddington.

associations of their homes will make them conversant with the habits and manners of gentlemen.

Consequently when these young men become station masters they also become 'Jacks in Office', and have seriously injured the old friendly feeling which existed between the public and the officials.

At the same time there is a considerable amount of importance attached to this public place of meeting—the railway station. The Jones's who don't associate with the Robinsons, meet there. Mr Jones would not like the station master to touch his cap to the Robinsons, and pass him without notice, so he sends the station master a hare. The Rev. Mr Silvertongue is always wanting to take a party somewhere at single fare for the double journey, or some other concession, so he honours the station master by conversing with him, as an equivalent for concessions.

The old lady with her dog would not, on any account, have the little dear put into that dreadful dungeon of a dog box when she travels, so she sends the station master a basket of plums once in the year.

The farmer would not like his teams of horses to be sent back without his oil cake or seed corn, for which he is waiting, in case he is not at home to write out a cheque for the carriage when he sends for the goods, so he sends a couple of rabbits about once in two years.

The grocer and other tradesmen want their claims for delay and damage (by which they hope to extort an additional profit) attended to, so they encourage the station master by standing treat whenever they meet him at the inn; or send a little box of French plums.

The doctor hopes to be sent for in case of a railway accident, so he is polite.

'My Lord' knows that he has no right to bully at the railway station, so he brings a brace of pheasants, and thus adds Mr Station Master to the train of his servants.

The old egg woman, who goes to market and takes a huge market basket in with her, which takes up the room of one passenger, ties up a few primroses and daffodils in a cabbage leaf, and hands them through the pigeon-hole when she takes her ticket.

The fish dealer, who is continually making claims for delay to his fish. drops a pair of soles, and when the station master says, 'How much'? he replies, 'We will settle for them when you pays me that claim, sir!'

The stockbroker hands his cigar case. In fact all but magistrates and the shareholders pay homage to the station master.

Owing to all these little circumstances combined, and with a staff of four men. I found myself quite a person of importance at Hinehoe Station, and very soon made myself at home, as everybody introduced themselves to me.

The old gentleman who acted as Agent to the Great Smash Company, and delivered the goods to the town of Dreddington,[1] offered me a ride in his covered spring van, and, being anxious to inspect the town, I accompanied him. The town was at that time a very old-fashioned place, and the appearance and customs have since entirely altered. One custom was for the chief tradespeople to meet every night at 'The Sow and Pigs' public-house and drink and sing songs. Save Saturday, business hours were from 6.0 a.m. to 4.0 p.m., at which hour the tradesmen usually put on their best bib and tucker, partook of an early cup of tea, and turned out for the evening.

It was to 'The Sow and Pigs' that Mr Tench took me, and I soon ascertained that I was not the only new public officer in the neighbourhood, for the customers were talking very disrespectfully about a Mr Williams, an Exciseman, who had recently come into the neighbourhood.

'What lies the fellow tells', observed a dry old customer in one corner, who was the pork butcher and bacon curer of the town, and who was reported to be worth £10,000. 'If he comes any of his stretchers to-night I'll give him one for himself.'

'Bravo !' and 'Well done, Mr Stubbles !' cried most of the others.

'It will do him good. Do give him one. Don't spare him', said another. 'I suppose, because he comes from a town where a few soldiers were kept, he takes us for country bumpkins.'

The object of their remarks soon stalked into the room, much to the delight of everyone present, and he must have felt flattered by the very patronizing manner in which most of those present said, 'Good evening, Mr Williams.'

The conversation turned upon dogs. Someone had been bitten by a dog, when Mr Williams took the lead and told us a little incident in connection with his own experience of dogs.

'It reminds me', he said, 'of a dawg one of the officers had. I used to mess with the officers, and one of them possessed the most ferocious brute you ever saw. It got loose on two occasions only. The first night it brought five sheep into Barracks, and the next time it captured a donkey and brought him in by the nose. Lord Cleverton, who owned the dawg, bet me that I would not face it. A wager was made and the dawg was brought in. The room was cleared. I placed myself in a corner, turned up my sleeves, and the dawg

[1] Deddington.

was loosed. He came at me in a most ferocious manner, but I met him with a tremendous kick, and he died on the spot. I knew where to kick the brute, and I won the wager.'

'Well done! well done! Mr Williams', said a dozen voices, and they began to look towards Mr Stubbles.

Mr Stubbles puffed away at his pipe as if in deep thought, and Mr Williams treated several of the tradesmen.

At last Mr Stubbles commenced his attack by saying, 'So you killed the dog, Mr Williams.'

'Yes', said that gentleman, 'dead as a stone.'

'That reminds me of a job I once had with a dog', said Mr Stubbles. 'If you gentlemen would like to hear it I will tell you.'

Everyone was very pressing for him to relate it, and foremost was Mr Williams.

'Well', said Mr Stubbles, 'it's no good hiding the fact, but I began business as a very poor man, and I used to go round with a basket to the farm houses.'

'No disgrace that', put in Mr Williams, 'A man's a man for a' that.'

'Well', continued Mr Stubbles, 'there was one farm house where there was a terribly savage sheep dog, who was always after me, and one day he popped round the corner and took a bit clean out of my trousers, behind. I didn't like this at all and I determined to be one with him. So one day I put my basket down and placed myself in a corner against the porch of the house, and I turned my sleeves up. The dog came at me and I rammed my hand down his throat, took hold of his tail, and turned him inside out. The dog ran away and looked *so* stupid. He never barked at me afterwards.'

Everyone laughed immensely but Mr Williams, who very soon wished us 'good evening'.

The people at the village of Hinehoe were most exemplary. It was one of those parishes where the squire ruled the parson, and the parson ruled the people. Any man who did not touch his hat to the parson and attend church was an outlaw, unworthy of soup tickets and parish relief, and if he fell ill he might get better as he could; but if, on the other hand, he was respectful in his conduct, and his wife picked up news or gossip for the curate, as to what his neighbours and their wives and families did—then he was a worthy man, and could afford to lose one day a week and spend it at a public house, whilst his wife went for soup and scraps to the mansion.

There was a spinster lady, who kept the curate's house, took in day scholars, and whose conduct, gait, and attire were a pattern to the village. This lady went occasionally to Snorum, to a library, to change books and to collect works for the Sunday School, and, being very precise, she invariably came to the Railway Station half-an-hour or more before the train started. On one occasion she came even earlier than usual, and made it quite a favour that I should give her a ticket, in order that she might cross the line and wait in the shed opposite for the train.

Of course I gave the ticket, and, seated on a form opposite, she was deeply absorbed in a book until the train came up.

Whether she was dreaming, or whether the book had carried her thoughts away, I cannot say, but certainly she made no movement to join the train until the engine whistled and the train started simultaneously. The whistle must have startled her, for she rushed to the train, and before any of us could get near her, she had caught hold of the handle of one of the carriage doors and had been dragged down between the train and the platform.

We all shouted to the driver to stop, and fortunately attracted his attention, although the train had got into a swing.

The poor lady was nowhere to be seen, and the train had by this time run quite fifty yards, with her travelling between the train and the brick wall of the platform. As the carriage which she had clutched emerged from the end of the platform we discovered that the lady had been dragged along, feet foremost, the whole distance, marvellous to say, uninjured. The slightest movement would have proved fatal; and the interval between her fall and the stoppage of the train was one of breathless suspense and anxiety to all who had witnessed the accident. The calmest individual on the spot was the lady herself, who, having adjusted her dress, which had been sadly disarranged by the event, looked round and exclaimed, 'Where's my pocket handkerchief?'

A passenger remarked, 'Hang your pocket handkerchief; you ought to thank God your life is spared', but this had no effect on her, and she insisted on the handkerchief being found before she would proceed (and it was found where she had fallen). So much for the *nerve of a spinster!*

Mr Peltum was in the habit of bringing his papers down to Hinehoe Station and writing all the morning in the waiting room. It was quiet, and he got through a lot of work with me as his secretary. You may be sure that I took advantage of the opportunity to enquire as to my prospect of an increase of pay.

'This sir', I said, 'makes four promotions with only one £10 rise. It is evident it can be different, or how can Mr Badger be appointed at £80 before he has been six months in the service? I had rather go back to Puzzle Junction, sir, at £70, for there I did go out sometimes, whereas here I lose the advantage of that.'

'Mr Stwuggles,' said Mr Peltum, 'compawisons are odious! but I pwomise you, Mr Stwuggles, that you shall be appointed to the fiwst £80 station that is vacant.'

I was obliged to put up with this, and I took a small farm house in a field near the station, where I not only made myself at home and bought some pigs and sheep, but I actually brought Mrs Struggles home to share my £70 per annum.

The occasion of my being married was the first holiday I had taken since I had been in the service of the Great Smash Railway, and then I only took two days, one to go to London and prepare, and the other to be married and return to Hinehoe. My wife was thoroughly domesticated and we got on very well. Fresh butter was 1s per lb., mutton 7d and 7½d per lb., and I produced my own vegetables. The rent of our little farm house was £6 per annum.

You must not imagine for one moment that my old friend Mr Calcraft, the auditor, had deserted me all this time. On the contrary, we had frequently met at the stations where I had been relieving, and at Puzzle Junction he had made a dead set at the £4 short in the four tickets I had undercharged, sending a full report to Mr Fretsum, and intimating that, as a beginner, I had possibly been short of cash and made use of the company's money. This charge I refuted by proving that I had £90 in the London and Westminster Bank when I joined the company.

Mr Mulberry believed that I had lost the money, and as I wrote to Mr Butcher, the director, explaining the matter and received a reply that he would see that justice was administered, Mr Fretsum and Mr Calcraft dropped the subject.

No sooner did Mr Calcraft hear of my marriage than he came down to Hinehoe, and clasping my hand, said, 'Ernest, I congratulate you. I came down on purpose to make the acquaintance of Mrs Struggles, but we must keep up the old practice—business first and pleasure afterwards.' He then went thoroughly into the books and accounts; made notes of several little irregularities which occurred during my two days' absence, and then honoured myself and wife with his presence.

One would have thought from his conversation to Mrs Struggles that he positively loved me, and as to her cooking—why, he never enjoyed anything so much in his life. I had married a perfect treasure, to whom he sung two songs, and related some of his domestic matters. His children—yes, his children; he was not vain, but he was proud to say they were all gifted. Mrs Struggles should see them some day.

The only return made for this entertainment was a very severe letter from Mr Fretsum about the omissions and inaccuracies that occurred during my two days' absence, and Mr Calcraft had omitted even to mention that it was owing to my absence they had occurred.

Christmas came, and with it a goose from Mr Wilson, a farmer close by. The goose was cooked and the appetite sharpened, when the telegraph instrument called me; 'Bother that telegraph!' It was not very pleasing when a nice goose was cooked, to be obliged to stop and take off a message for the squire. To find when you had taken it off, the men had all decamped to their dinners, with the exception of the signalman, who could not be sent away. To have to deliver the message yourself and wait for an answer, which the squire wanted sent immediately, and then, on your return to have to call for half-an-hour before you could attract attention at the station the message was for, who told you to 'wait, he was engaged,' finally to arrive home two hours late for dinner, to find the little wife almost crying, and the goose dried up; and yet this was my first family Christmas dinner.

'What station is this?' said a commercial traveller as a train pulled up.

'*Ino*', said a porter who spoke through his nose and could not say 'Hinehoe.'

'*You know*, you blockhead, I daresay you do know, but I want to know. Where's the station master?'

The porter who spoke through his nose called me. I answered the enquiry and the train passed on.

Whilst we were attending to this train on the opposite side a police inspector drove to the station, and, taking advantage of our absence, he tried all the weights and scales which were used for weighing the goods and the parcels. It was a very unfair thing to do in our absence, and we all thought so.

On my return he strode into my office and addressed himself to me as follows:

'Your weights and scales are wrong. I intend to report them.'

I simply bowed.

'What is your name?'

This gentleman was a Scotchman, and his bearing and manner were altogether domineering and offensive.

'My name is over the door', I replied, 'but, as I am not a felon, I will trouble you to walk out of this office.'

'You are rather cool, young man, but I will bring you to book,' said the inspector.

In a few days I was served with a summons to appear at Middle Bar[1] for

[1] Banbury.

defrauding the public. I communicated with Mr Peltum, who provided me with a solicitor to defend me, or rather the company, and I appeared.

There were two magistrates, one a good sort of fox-hunting Conservative squire, and the other was the Rev. Mr Witchfield, a regular Tartar.[1] Not content with fining the company, he attacked me for being rude to the inspector.

The other magistrate would not admit this last charge, as he certainly thought the inspector should have first applied to me, and as regards my name, he should have known where to find it. The company too, appealed against the Rev. Mr Witchfield's decision, because the machine questioned was a spring balance, and weighed correctly if only the dial hand was adjusted at the time of weighing. They carried the case to another court, and the charge was ultimately dismissed, but it occasioned me a great deal of trouble and anxiety.

My house and garden were just put in good order when I had offer of another station at £80 per annum. We were anxious to get on in the railway world so I accepted it, and we packed up and removed to Fame station.[2]

---

[1] Perhaps the Rev. F. Litchfield of Farthinghoe.
[2] Thame.

## CHAPTER VII

*Fame Station—My Good Neighbour—Tom Burley, the Porter—The Old Woman's First and Last Ride by Train—A Mistake with the Train Staff and a John Gilpin's Ride to recover it—Mad Sandy*

THREE years had been spent in the service of the Great Smash Company, and I had arrived at the enormous sum of £80 per annum, and had been moving about the whole time, like one who collects tolls at a turnpike, but I flatter myself that I had learnt my business.

Fame Station was a terminus, and situate in a market town.[1] So far it was more lively, and we obtained a nice little house for £8 per annum, with a garden and the right of a run into a woodyard, and orchard. This orchard was used as a timber yard, and we were never short of chips to light the fires. The landlord was a quaint old chap, and used to come occasionally and smoke a long pipe and drink gin and water with us, and then tell us to help ourselves to the chips.

He was a reported miser himself, and had a lunatic sister confined upstairs at his own house, and having no wife or child, I think he liked a little change sometimes. He was peculiar, but kind, and whenever he met me away from the station he invariably paused, and smiling, made some jocular remark, such as this—'Well, young man, I never see you without thinking you are a marvel. No sign of any whisker, and here you are in charge of a station and a wife. You must have a nerve!'

Our next door neighbour was Abel Valley, the cattle dealer, and he was the man to keep you from over-sleeping. About 4.0 a.m. in the summer he commenced sorting his horned cattle and sheep, just underneath our bedroom window, with the aid of his bob-tailed black sheep dog, 'Bob.'

If you were asleep you were very soon roused, with cries of 'Gu along round 'em, Bob. That ull do, that ull do', combined with Bob's barking, and the cows bellowing or sheep bleating. It was useless to think of getting

[1] The line from High Wycombe to Thame was opened on 1 August 1862.

off to sleep again, so I got up and worked at my garden, or helped Abel Valley sort his cattle.

We very soon became fast friends, and his sister, a very kind old lady, was like a mother to my wife.

Abel would say, 'I say, Master Struggles, when you come home to-night just pop in and write a letter or two for me, cos you knows I aint no scholard, and then I'll look you out two or three nice heifers to graze out this summer, that will pay you some money.'

It was no trouble to me write Abel's letters, which were for the most part something to this effect.

'Sir,

'I have been expecting a cheque from you for the hundred sheep supplied last March. I understand you have sold the wool, and sold the sheep to another man, without even giving me the offer. Now you know this is not business, and not serving me right after trusting you, when your swedes was all running away, and you couldn't find anybody to find you sheep to feed them off, to get your barley in. I beg to say that unless you meet me next market day and settle I shall put you into my lawyer's hands.

'I remain, yours truly,

'ABEL VALLEY.'

It was no good my trying to alter the composition—although it was somewhat remarkable for a field of swedes to run away, or a creditor to be placed into a lawyer's hands.—A letter thus written gave immense satisfaction to Abel, who would exclaim, 'That ul do 'im, Mr Struggles, that ul do 'm. I wish I was a scholard, I wouldn't begrudge a flock of ship. What ul you 'ave, Mr Struggles?'

Abel had a nice garden too, and many a basket of nice fruit was sent in to Mrs Struggles by his sister, Mrs Clayton.

I took advantage of Abel's offer to let me have some heifers, and invested all my money in cattle, which I placed out to 'joist' as they called it, that was, to graze at so much per head during the summer. Indeed, if it had not been for Abel's help, I cannot say how we should have made both ends meet on £80 per annum, for troubles were in store for us.

The town was one of the cleanest, nicest country towns I ever lived in. The street was four times the width of ordinary streets, and the people were thrifty and prosperous.

A large cattle market was held in its centre every week, and an auctioneer, who put us in mind of a very fast talking parrot, did an extraordinary stroke of business on a stool in the centre of the market. Mounted on his stool he sold cows, oxen, and bulls with immense rapidity, and invariably wound up his recapitulation of bids, 21, 22, 23, 24, by saying, 'Shan't dwell about her', although it might be a bull he was selling, and down went the hammer.

The chief hotel was the 'Falcon.'[1] It was a fine building with every accommodation for the coaches which formerly ran that way. It boasted of an omnibus which met the trains, a billiard table, commercial room, carriages and horses to let; and the landlord was proprietor, brewed his own beer, had a brickyard, and delivered goods for the Great Smash Company. Altogether Mr Simens, the landlord of the 'Falcon', was a most important man in the town. He was more like the Emperor of Germany than any man I ever saw, gentlemanly in his manners, John Bull in his style, but possessed of a most hasty temper.

At first I thought his life quite an enviable one, but I soon ascertained that there was a skeleton in his house. He had a daughter by his first wife, whose intellect was weak. He had married a widow with four children, whose property he needed to release the encumbrances on his own, and the executors had placed the matter in Chancery instead of handing him the cash. Mrs Simens was indeed a quaint old body. She was very stout, not tall, and invariably wore a black silk dress both summer and winter. This good lady was always in the bar, ornamented with curls and jewellery, and her manners were of the most simpering nature. She called her husband 'Pappa, dear', and her two daughters who were at home, 'Emma, dear', and 'Jenny, dear.' Her son had emigrated out of the way of 'Pappa dear's' wrath, and her oldest daughter had made a runaway match. The two remaining daughters followed their dear mother's example and simpered to everybody, more especially to collegians and commercial travellers, to whom they did not object to play and sing, but at the slightest liberty on the part of either they would rise majestically, and saying, 'I thought you were a gentleman', would sail off to mama dear, when mama would appear and say, 'Well, Mr Cocoanut, I really *am* astonished!' Mr Cocoanut would then pay a visit to his grocers for orders and when he came back Emma dear and Jenny dear had forgotten all about the little kiss that was proffered, and they played and sang again.

The work at the station was single-handed and hard. I had enough to do. My predecessor, Mr Giant, was, without exception, the best railway man I ever met with. He had been promoted to Byfield Station.[2] His books were in perfect order, and he had written on one of the fly leaves of his

---

[1] The Eagle, later more famous as the Spread Eagle.

[2] Twyford.

cash book that the chief qualifications for a railway man were 'accuracy and despatch'. No one possessed these qualifications so exactly, to my mind, as himself. Although the work was hard I managed to get through it, upon the old maxim, that 'if you want any thing done well, do it yourself', I had very few errors to correct, and therefore little annoyance from the Audit Office. Mr Calcraft was supplied with butter, eggs, and poultry, from this station, which were sent free of carriage, and so was my district superintendent, Mr Whirlpool. They sent a note each week as to what I was to buy and forward, and Mr Whirlpool had his butcher's meat from Fame, which was purchased cheaper by 1½d and 2d per lb. than at Plough,[1] where Mr Whirlpool resided.

I had quite a strong commission, what with meat, butter, eggs, and poultry to buy for these people weekly, for which I never received even thanks, although Tom Burley, the porter, who came to market with me, always expected a pint of ale for collecting the things, but Tom was a worthy fellow and I never begrudged him his pint of beer. He had been sent to me as a new hand, and was a most apt pupil.

Mr Whirlpool was a good looking tall man, about 35 years of age. He wat the son of the Steward of one of the chief shareholders—Sir somebody, and he was what might be termed 'a fast man about town.'

At a recent race-meeting the grand stand fell and he with it, by which misadventure he was laid up for some months, and a Mr Levant,[2] his neighbouring superintendent, undertook to look to his district.

Mine being a terminus, from which there was no chance of his returning for at least three hours, he very rarely paid me a visit, and I reigned almost supreme at Fame station. As I went to and from my house to the station the little boys in the street used to say, 'That's the station master,' and on Sunday quite a tribe of country people walked in to see the trains start, for the railway was only just opened, and very few country people had travelled by a train. Our engine driver, for we had only one, had quite extinguished their admiration of 'the Village Blacksmiths', and, as our station was worked as a branch line from Fitzboro'[3] to Fame, the plough boys saved up their money and had a ride from Fame to Fitzboro' on a Sunday, for the novelty of the thing. I have booked as many as fifty of these youngsters on one Sunday, who had no other object in travelling.

---

[1] Slough.

[2] Besant, afterwards Divisional Superintendent, Swansea.

[3] Apparently Princes Risborough (in the key, and cf. p. 98), though the pseudonym is more appropriate to High Wycombe, a borough dominated by the Marquess of Lansdowne, whose surname was Petty Fitzmaurice.

My first pantomime did not delight me more than this ride delighted them, and they walked back eight and nine miles to whistle and plough, and talk about 'how the trees and hedges rund alongh when "us" was in that thaire train', and how 'it frit I, when she went under the arch.'

Abel's propensity for sorting sheep was not confined to week days, indeed, when there was a fair in the neighbourhood, Abel repaired thither and then we rejoiced in a peaceful slumber some week days, but so sure as Sunday morning came, Bob, the sheep dog, and his master were at work from 4 a.m. to 7 a.m., after which Abel shaved, dressed himself, and read the Bible, although he never went to Church.

This Sunday morning performance suited me, for I had a train to start at 6.45 a.m., which was the only train out until 4 p.m., and as I could not work in my garden on Sunday, and did not care to help sort sheep in my Sunday togs, I repaired to the station and made up my weekly accounts without interruption. Not so one Sunday morning, for a gentle tap at the station door told me I had a visitor. To my surprise, too, it was a female, and as I opened the door the neatest, cleanest, and most respectable old countrywoman I ever chanced to meet walked in and curtseyed to me.

To describe my visitor—she was about 50 years of age; her bonnet was a plain straw, with about three pieces of ribbon across it—it was one of that sensible kind of bonnet which keeps the ears warm and projects quite six inches over the forehead; her dress was a very clean cotton print without any fulness, and very short, which, together with her thick strong boots, gave her a school-girl look below; a large shawl, mostly yellow, fastened with a large common pin, completed her attire.

'Good marning, sir; bin you the station master?' said my visitor.

I assured her that I was, when she continued—

'Please, sir, I be going by train, and do you know, sir, I've never bin. I *do hope* I shall go safe! I be going to Ducktown[1] to see my darter Betty, and she's a comin down by the Long and Narrow Railway,[2] and we be going to spend the day there at a sister's as I've got, and then she's a going back to sarvice, and I be a coming home; and I do hope, sir, as you'll see me safe, for I be most afraid on't.'

Poor old soul, she trembled all over, so I took her into the waiting room and bade her sit down; but she reminded me of my own sittings in a dentist's room, when waiting to have a tooth out, for she was evidently ill at ease.

---

[1] Aylesbury.

[2] The London & North Western Railway.

I enquired how it was that no one came with her on this first occasion of her travelling, when she replied—

'Lor bless 'e, sir! my 'usband's the fogger[1] at the farm, and he can't no more get away a Sundays nor he could a week days, for he's got all the cattle to do morn and night, and the fatting things three times. He never went away only once, and then one of the bullocks got blowed up, hoved like. And as to my sister what lives in the village, why she wunt go nowhere nighst them trains. She wunt even go to look at them, for she says it's agen the will o' God to run a coach wi'out osses, and as my darter Betty writ to say as she's bin by 'em times, and there aint no 'arm, I be comed all alone, but I do wish, sir, as I was a going in a waggin and osses, I should be safe there.'

Of course I bade my friend sit still, told her to banish all idea of fear, and make herself comfortable where she was.

'Thank you, sir, you be a kind sort of a genelman,' replied my friend, and I returned to my labours, closing my office door. Very few moments, however, elapsed before the old lady knocked at the door, and stating that she was so 'hunkied' (this means dull), begged to be allowed to sit in my office. I could not refuse her, and her first enquiry was, 'Please, sir, do you tickut me here, or when I gets there?'

I explained the process of ticket taking, when she next said, 'Please, sir, will you show me where I 'aves to get in?'

There was nothing for it but to banish all idea of work and show the old lady on to the platform.

Once there she stared about like a newly captured bird. The first matter which attracted her attention was the railroad itself, and gazing at the iron rails she caught hold of my sleeve and said, 'Lar', sir, it bee wonderful, baint it! Do it run along inside them iron things!'

I tried to enlighten her, but she turned her attention to the advertisements on the platform saying, 'What a many pretty pictures you 'ave got, sir!' Selecting one of the largest of the advertisements with a drawing of some large house of business, she remarked, with reference to it 'Some gurt genelmun's 'ouse I s'pose, sir?' I said, 'Yes', and she passed on to the Guano advertisement, with a penguin sitting on a rock, and she said, 'That be very pretty! some kind of a duck, sir, I s'pose?'

Having given her directions, I took her back to the office, gave her a ticket and instructions as to changing trains at Fitzboro' Junction for Ducktown. This produced fresh terror in the old lady's mind, who said,

[1] A farm-labourer concerned with cattle.

'Oh dear, oh dear, I wish I'd never com'd! I do hope I shall go safe!'

To my infinite delight the guard who had to work the train came earlier than he was wont to do, and to his care I handed over this lady passenger, who followed him about, up and down, and in and out, much to his annoyance, until the train came in.

When the train arrived she tried to escape from the platform and backed into the booking office, but catching sight of me she clutched me and I found she was trembling violently.

'Lar, sir,' said she, 'I thought *he* was a going to bust up' (meaning the engine).

I showed her to a carriage, and directing her not to change at the first station but the next, I wished her 'good morning.'

'Good marnin, sir, and thenk 'e. Not to change at the first station but the next, I do 'ope I shall gu safe', was the last I heard of her, and the train started.

I confess I felt bored, for although somebody says, 'You can't have too much of a good thing', yet I had done no work through the old lady's nonsense, and I made haste to accomplish my usual duties before the train came back with its freight from Fitzboro' Junction, after which I was free until 4 p.m.

I had just finished when the train was signalled, and I walked out to meet it.

Nothing unusual occurred until I noticed an old woman get out of the train so like the one I had despatched, that I had the curiosity to walk towards her. There was the coal-scuttle bonnet, the yellow shawl, the scant dress, and the same boots.

Could it be possible that the old lady despatched had changed and rechanged at the Junction until she had accidentally got into the wrong train, and come back to Fame instead of going to Ducktown? Yes, it was so; and as she sighted me she cast the most woeful look, and putting both hands up, exclaimed—

'Lor' me, I be at Fame again, and my darter Betty's at Ducktown!'

You may be sure that I blamed the Guard, but he said that to begin with, she rushed out at the first station, and that he had to stop the train to get her in again; that when he got to Fitzboro' Junction he took her and told her where to wait; that then he had his parcels and milk cans to see to, and that it was not his fault if she rushed about like a maniac at the sound of every whistle, and made a fool of herself. He did not see her in his train or he should have been only too glad to get rid of her.

Poor old thing, she cried bitterly; waited all day at the station, and went again by the four o'clock train, on which occasion I booked her as a parcel, putting a label on her umbrella, and handing the guard a way bill of 'One woman for Ducktown.'

She found her daughter, spent two hours with her, and returned by the last train, but vehemently declared as she went home, 'Never no more trains for me, if I can't go in a waggin I'll stay at home till I be berrid, that I will.'

Mr. Levant, the temporary superintendent, paid me a visit about this time. He was a manly, well disposed gentleman, had been a sailor, and did not scruple to smoke his pipe and tell you what he thought.

'Struggles', said he, 'You have got rather an easy time of it here. Plenty of work, I admit, but no express trains, and no Directors passing.'

I replied that I should prefer these things to working single line with a staff and tickets, and that I hoped if he had a vacancy in his district he would think of me, as I should like to be on the main line again. He promised to do so.

To those of my readers who do not understand what working single line with a staff and tickets is, I will endeavour to explain.

Single line is where there is only one line for both up and down trains, and to prevent those trains meeting, a staff is instituted, and unless that staff is *at the Station* no guard or driver dares start a train. To this staff is attached a key which unlocks a box containing tickets, on which was printed, 'Train Ticket, Staff to follow', so that so long as the staff is at the station any number of trains may be despatched, but directly the staff itself is despatched with a train, all power to start trains goes with it to the next station, where the same key unlocks a similar box of tickets, and the other station master many start any number of trains until he too gives up the staff.

Of course you can readily imagine that by some trains it is necessary to send a ticket in order that a second train may follow, and by some trains it is necessary to send the staff in order that a train may come in. I used to dream about this staff, and well I might, for the slightest error was 'a Board Job.'

Living in the town was a horse dealer, named Tower, who collected and sold horses for the French Government. He took to me because he had bought two good young horses of my father, and because I could converse in French with the gentleman who came to inspect his horses. In fact he said, 'Mr Struggles, when you want to shake your liver up, come to me and I'll give you a mount.'

It was not long before this railway staff occasioned me to apply to him.

One day I forwarded the staff by a train as usual, forgetting there was an additional train that month, for which I should have detained the staff. It was not until the train was out of sight that I thought of it, and then, without a word to the porters, I ran into the town to secure a horse to ride eight miles to Fitzboro' Junction to get it back in time for the next train.

Mr Tower was at home, and in answer to my request for the promised mount he replied, 'Very sorry, my boy, but I haven't a horse in that you you can ride. The only horse we have in the stable is a colt, and my son has been on him once. I wouldn't trust him out for a gold watch.'

Someone called him away, and with beating heart and visions of 'Up before the Board', I went into the stable, hoping to find that he had made a mistake and that I should find another horse. There stood only the colt, and there hung the saddle and the breaking bit. Mr Tower did not return. It was 'of two evils choose the least.' There was a side way of escape with the colt, and in a few moments it would be too late. Many a colt I had assisted my elder brother to break in at home, and all my 'Rarey'[1] propensities were revived at the moment. The colt was saddled and bridled and I was on him. I got him out of the stable and out of the yard unobserved, and I made for Fitzboro' Junction at the shigshag trot of an unbroken colt.

Looking at my watch I saw there was no time to lose. How thankful I was to get out of the town and to escape observation in order that I might accelerate the pace of the raw recruit I was riding.

At last, by means of shouting 'Hoop up', and sundry sharp cuts on his thigh and shoulders with a long ash stick I had borrowed from the stable, he broke into a canter, and I began to see hopes of escape from attending the Board of Directors, supported by that ever memorable picture of their late secretary, when the colt plunged, reared, and nearly fell backwards with me.

Under ordinary circumstances I should have said 'Whoa, lad!' and pulled him up, but these were extraordinary circumstances. It was 'neck or nothing', and I believe that at that moment I could have ridden a wild stag. All consideration for the poor animal was out of the question. It was 'Time', 'Railway-staff', 'Board', and when the colt alighted, whack went the ash stick on his near thigh, as only those accustomed to rough riding can plant it.

To my infinite delight he struck into a gallop and once more I felt at home. Faster he galloped. I rose in the stirrups and fairly cried, 'Hurrah', when the truth dawned upon me—he had run away. Madly he dashed along

---

[1] Rarey was a famous horse-breeder. See the *Oxford English Dictionary*.

that narrow road, fortunately meeting no one. His hoofs clattered and the agricultural labourers ran towards the hedge to catch a sight of me riding like John Gilpin of old, but they were all too late, for we had passed before their clumsy efforts had brought them to the road, and for full four miles we continued this headlong career.

Already I could see the railway signals about a mile on my side of the station, when my steed made a sudden swerve, shot up a green lane to a gate, and neighed.

It was not the spirited neigh of the horse; it was the conquered neigh of the vanquished colt, which they invariably send forth when they are overcome.

I was nearly unhorsed by the sudden turn, and before I could turn my steed, he laid down on the turf.

Here was a pretty fix. Should I run to the station and return to my colt, but then, where would he be on my return, for you cannot tie up unbroken colts with bridles, they will break twenty bridles one after another, besides there was not time to run, and I began to despair when I recollected that I had a box of vesuvian matches[1] in my pocket. I struck about six of these at once and suddenly applying them to his nostrils, up jumped my steed, but he had decided not to allow me to remount. Round and round we went, I trying to get my foot into the stirrup, he trying to prevent me. Then I led him to the gate, placed his head over it, and, before he could turn I had remounted. He was then under perfect control and we soon reached Fitzboro' Junction Station. I got a boy to hold my horse and hurried into the station. Not a soul was there, and a sparrow flew out of the booking office as I entered.

There hung the staff. Not for long, for in an instant it was in my pocket, a penny was paid to the boy, and we were homeward bound. My colt behaved admirably, trotted and cantered by turns, and four minutes to the appointed time of the train's starting I had shut him in the cattle pen behind the goods shed, and I walked leisurely into the booking office at Fame station as if nothing had happened. The people were a little uneasy about their tickets it is true, but there were not more than twelve of them. They were soon booked and I was about to start the train when Tom Burley came rushing into the office like a wild man.

'Mr Struggles', said he, 'I've bin to your house and all over the town for you. Do you know, sir, you sent the staff away by that last train, and that this un can't start? I see you give it to the guard.'

---

[1] Matches that ignited with a sputtering flame, used for lighting cigars and pipes in the open air.

'Nonsense', I replied, at the same time producing it from my pocket. Tom Burley stared like one in a trance.

'Thank God for that', said Tom, but he never moved, and after I had started the train I found him still standing with his fingers in his hair, as if thunderstruck.

'Sir', said he, 'I could have laid my life as you sent that staff away. I've bin to your house, and to every place where I thought you'd be, to find you. Where was you, sir?'

'Don't make a noise', I replied, 'come with me and clean this horse.'

Poor horse, he was one mass of white foam.

I unsaddled him and led him into the goods shed, whilst Tom knocked an iron hoop off an old barrel, with which we scraped him all over, to get the perspiration out of his coat. We then rubbed him with loose litter and straw, and finally brushed him with a birch broom and walked him about until he was dry. This done, Tom re-saddled him and took him home the back way and re-placed him as I had directed.

Only one person at the station did I let into the secret of my being scarcely able to walk for some days, and that person was Tom Burley, whose admiration for my exploit was constantly showing itself in some small, but kindly manner. He would not let me move from the office stool if he could help it, and the most remarkable thing connected with this adventure was that neither did the owner of the horse know that I had ridden his colt, for I made a confidant of his son who disguised it, nor did the station master at Fitzboro' Junction know that I had removed the staff. It so happened that he did not meet the next train, and the porter who met it received the staff and placed it in its usual position as a matter of course. Tom Burley and I had the joke to ourselves, but he often commented on it by saying, 'What fools they were at Fitzboro' Junction', or that, 'he would back that colt did not want much more breaking in.'

I was content to hear nothing, for 'where ignorance was bliss 'twas folly to be wise', and this was the first and last mistake I ever made with the staff.

James Sandy, our branch engine driver, was a troublesome man. He was quick, obliging, and above the average of engine drivers, so far as intelligence was concerned, but he had some dreadful failings, for he was fond of beer, fond of showing off with his engines, fond of mischief, had a dreadful habit of procrastination, was very hasty, and never saw danger. Smith, the guard who always accompanied James Sandy, or 'Mad Sandy', as the men called him, was very often complaining to me about him, and many a lecture I read Sandy.

Sandy would promise to be more steady, and would attribute Smith's complaining to the fact of his being in a consumption, usually winding up such lectures by saying,, 'Ah, sir, I'm not so bad as you make out. Them consumptive people is always a grumping and a growling!'

Sandy would reform for about three days, after which he would bring me a bundle of watercress gathered from a spring a few miles up the line, at which spot, in the face of all orders, he would pull up a goods train and let it stand on the line whilst he gathered the watercress. I did not know of this last irregularity for some time, otherwise I should have refused the cress.

The guard was not the only person Sandy worried, for there was a poor old crossing keeper two miles distant, whose tales of Sandy's mad conduct would fill a book, and who related some of the most hair breadth escapes people and farmers' wagons had experienced whilst crossing the line.

This poor old man, who was so feeble that he had great difficulty in walking to the station for his money, had once been a farmer in prosperous circumstances, but he was so reduced that he was glad to live in a miserable hut with his poor old wife, and mind the crossing for ten shillings per week. When I could spare the time I walked up with his money and some little trifle, and the old gentleman would tell me how he had hunted in scarlet, and how his poor old wife had entertained people, but he generally returned to his old grievance about Sandy, and these were the last words he spoke to me:

'Ah, sir, I know how 'twill be some day with that Mad Sandy, he never takes notice of my signal, and he will run into us and kill us, gate and all, some day.'

So long as 'Mad Sandy' was the only driver on the line there was no fear of his doing much damage, but the traffic increased and a new line was in course of construction from Fame to Snorum; a ballast train was already at work, and special arrangements made for its running.

One beautiful light evening we were waiting for this ballast train to come in, so that Sandy's train might proceed, when I heard the whistle of Sandy's engine. The passengers were all in the train, some forty or fifty of them, and Smith, the guard, was 'waiting signal' from me. At first I thought Sandy was running his engine up and down to pump water into her, as he was wont to do, but as it was rather unusual for him to do so at this time I stepped out of the office to satisfy myself. Merciful heaven! he had started with the train load of passengers, and without the guard, to certain death, for the ballast train was not in. All the men ran wildly after the train shouting, and I ran past them all and only just failed to jump on the step of the brake van, but our shouts and our exertions were of no avail, for, as usual, 'Mad Sandy' let off an enormous quantity of steam, which deafened all sound to him.

My legs failed me, and I sank on the embankment like one who has lost all hope.

Each awful moment we expected to hear the death crash, and we looked from man to man, all pictures of despair. As the moments—which were hours to us—wore on we were encouraged to hope.

'I know', said I, 'if he only gets round Towzer Corner[1] there is a straight road of four miles. He will see the other train coming and they will be saved. But go you, Tom Burley, and ask both doctors of the town to come *in case.*'

We walked on in silence, when, with horror together, we distinctly heard the death warning echo of the two brake whistles of the engines.

We paused and listened for the dreadful crash. The brake whistles ceased, and a shrill 'common whistle' told us that one train was about to start again.

'They are saved!' one and all exclaimed, and there was not a man there down whose cheeks the tears of thankfulness—which memory, even now, revives as I write—were not flowing copiously.

But how fared it with the dear old man at the crossing? He never lived to tell the tale, but his poor old wife, whose claim on the company was disregarded, and who is probably now in want, told me all about it.

'Poor dear man', she said, 'he was planting some seeds and had taken off the signal for the ballast train to come along when he looked up and saw Mad Sandy's train coming. I looked up and saw the ballast train coming too, and we both ran. Poor dear man, he shut the gate, not that it would stop the train, but he thought they might see it. He moved the large signal backwards and forwards and I waved the red flag. The ballast train blew the brake whistle and then Mad Sandy began to blow, but he couldn't stop much, because there was no guard in his train to put on the brake. The trains got quite near and we only just got in the house when Mad Sandy's train dashed right through the gate, and a large piece of the gate knocked that hole in the wall, where the poor dear man lays dead. Oh, Mr Struggles, they pulled up not ten yards from one another, and my dear husband said, "Thank God!" and fell back. He never spoke again, and I wish I had died with him.'

---

[1] Presumably the gentle curve in the line east of Towersey; but the topographical description is not exact.

Summary measures were taken against Mad Sandy, the engine driver. He was removed to be again the driver of a shunting engine at Snorum Station, and I venture to say that had he belonged to any other department but the locomotive he would have been dismissed the service.

Mr Whirlpool, too, made several visits to Fame and pried into my affairs. He attacked me as follows one day: 'Mr Struggles, I am told you deal in cattle. Am I rightly informed?'

Now I did not *deal* in cattle, I simply expended my little capital for the summer, and as I did not think it was any business of his, and as I had heard that he was in the habit of betting at race meetings rather largely, I made the following reply: 'You should not believe all you hear, sir, for instance, someone was unkind enough to say to me that you betted rather largely the other day.' This was quite sufficient for Mr Whirlpool and he never referred to my little speculations again, but he was exceedingly sharp with me.

The Fame people clamoured loudly for the new line to be opened to Snorum, which expected event was to be an immense boon, but which has, in reality, worked against them by bringing the trade of the town into competition with that of a much larger one, and by affording means of escape for commercial travellers and others who were obliged in the old days to stay the night.

Railways drain small towns and feed large ones.

At last the happy day arrived.[1] A communication from Mr Peltum requested that I would order a hot luncheon for six gentlemen, to include Mr O'Reilly, the London Traffic Superintendent, Mr Whirlpool, and himself.

At the time appointed Mr O'Reilly, two Directors, the contractor who had made the line, Mr Whirlpool, and Mr Gabriel Gouge arrived. They came up the new line from Snorum Station, and I met them, hoping that I should be invited to luncheon, or that, at the very least, they would crack a bottle of wine to drink success to the new line.

Vain hope! No one took the slightest notice of me, and I followed the party about as if I were a black slave.

A great deal was said about the gradients. How many hundred yards more ballast would be required, and where it was to come from, and how many weeks a train would have to run to bring this ballast. That there must be some more signals, another crossing, and a siding.

Mr Gouge was requested to caution the drivers until the line was properly

---

[1] The line from Thame to Oxford was opened on 25 October 1864.

ballasted and the signals completed, but there was no necessity for the opening to be delayed, and the trains were to run next day as advertised, and they did.

Nothing was said about any additional staff to assist me with the working of this new line, and I was not consulted about a single matter.

At last Mr O'Reilly called me, and with a bland smile handed me Mr Peltum's overcoat from the saloon carriage in which they had arrived. 'Struggles', said he, 'Mr Peltum was called back after we started, and left his coat, book it back to him as a parcel. We are going the other way. Put the saloon on the 4 o'clock train for us.'

I took the coat, and felt that at last I had something to do, although it was only the custody of an old rusty overcoat, when Mr O'Reilly called me back.

'Here', said he, as if he was addressing a dog, 'this brake carriage is going back to Snorum. Put the coat in here.'

'Perhaps, sir', I ventured to remark, 'I had better book it to ensure its safe transit.'

'You do as I tell you; quite enough for you to do', roared Mr O'Reilly.

I dropped the coat and walked away, and this was the only part I played in the opening of the new line.

Family troubles speedily arrived, and, although I could not boast of much whisker, I was very soon to boast of an offspring, and presently a nurse and a doctor took possession of Mrs Struggles and the keys of the cupboards.

Hour after hour and day after day I expected to be received on my return from the station with the glad tidings 'that it was all over and that so and so', but after incessant visits from the doctor and his partner I was requested to step into our little parlour 'to see the doctor.'

'Mr Struggles', said he, 'your little son is dead, and I cannot say that your wife will survive, but we will do our best.'

With this intelligence, and without permission to visit the sick room, I mournfully retraced my steps to the station, for there were more trains now, and there was more anxiety.

I had no proper signalman, and the duty of shifting the signals devolved on a porter, named 'Broom', a young man, who had several other duties, whose negligence was often the subject of remonstrance from me.

The new line was already used as a short cut for an express goods train, which ran through our station 'full steam.'

The passenger train from Fitzboro' to Snorum stood on a side line whilst the express goods ran through, and after it had passed, the points communicating with the main line were opened and the passenger train proceeded.

Thus it depended on the closing or opening of these points as to the line on which the approaching express goods train ran.

My readers will thus be enabled to see that had these points been left open the approaching train would run into the passenger train standing on that side line, instead of running safely through the station.

These points were a matter of great anxiety to me, for they were always being opened and shut for the ballast train, and I knew that 'Porter Broom', who had the care of them, was not to be depended upon.

That day I was booking the train and brooding over my troubles at home, when 'Broom' came in with his goods consignment notes. I never saw 'Broom' without refreshing his memory, and, from habit I suppose, I said to him, 'Have you put that signal right [for there was only one signal instead of two] for the express goods?'

'Yes, sir', replied Broom.

'And did you put the points right and lock them?' I further enquired.

'They were right this morning', replied Broom.

Not a moment's hesitation, not a second thought or enquiry, I did not even stop to close my cash drawer, but I knocked a passenger over who stood in the way of my shoulder, and I was running, not for my life, but for the lives of others, to the points, for I knew that if Broom had not put them right *since* the morning they must be wrong. The signal was indeed 'all right', but the points were 'all wrong', and the safety of the unconscious load of passengers depended on my turning them before the express train got there. She was coming 'full steam' and I was going 'full steam.' Broom, too, was coming behind me, but I had distanced him, for I could run.

If you had been an observer of the race I think you would have decided against my chance of success, but the excitement of the moment lent me the wings of lightning, as it were.

The train was coming like a charge of cavalry, the points were between us. I had to stand on the line where the train would pass if I missed the handle. It was death or victory.

Another moment and I should have been a mangled corpse or the train would have passed the station in safety.

I need not tell you that it was the latter, I had turned the points and had staggered backwards into a muddy ditch from which Broom extricated me, for my strength had gone.

It was three days before I fairly shook off the reaction of that run for life, and by that time my wife's life was out of danger.

A distressing letter from Phiz, at Puzzle Junction, informed me that he was in sad trouble. The sum of £20 was missing from his cash drawer.

He had been suspended, and before the Directors. The Directors heard his case, and they heard what Mr Mulberry had to say about him.

Finally they decided that Phiz might take his choice of two courses, viz., to pay the £20 and resign his situation, or to resist it and they would prosecute him and apply to his guarantee.

Poor Phiz was heartbroken and afraid to go home.

I wrote to him to come to me immediately, as Mr Simens was in want of a young man as brewer and correspondent.

I laid the whole facts before Mr Simens, adding my own opinion of the honesty of my late fellow clerk.

Mr Simens believed me and engaged him.

Phiz served him well, and has since prospered in the world.

He often paid me a visit at the station, and one of our chief amusements was Master Bull, a farmer's son, and a daily visitor to the station.

Master Bull came twice daily from a distant farm to bring milk to send to London. He was a fine uncultivated youth of about eighteen summers, but neither nature nor art had been bountiful to him, for he was not nice-looking, and not well clad. His outer garment was a green smock frock, his trousers nearly up to his knees, and his boots were very thick and heavy, his shirt collar was part and parcel of his blue shirt and only changed weekly, and his hat was a Dudley slouch hat, with a coat of cows' hair on its top, which had doubtless accumulated from his sticking his head into the cows' flanks to milk them.

Moreover his hands were chapped, and his hair was fiery-red, long, and hung like candles round his forehead.

In one respect he was an example to many, for Master Bull never spoke unless he was spoken to, and then he confined his conversation to the question put, but he laughed incessantly and immoderately at the smallest matter, with a 'haw, haw, haw.'

Master Bull was good natured, and if any of the men did anything out of the way for him he used to say, 'Brought ye a bottle of milk. Let me have the bottle back, mind.'

The men liked him, and I liked him. He walked about the station a privileged 'original', but obedient as a lamb.

'Now then, young Bull, hook it' ! said Tom Burley, 'I want you and your cart out of the way. The omnibus will be down directly.'

'I baint a going', said Bull, 'I've tied my cart up t'other side.'

'Not going', said Tom, 'what's up then ?'

'Oh, *I knows*', said Bull.

'And so do I', said Tom Burley, 'Don't you, Sir ?' addressing me.

I said, 'I suppose you are afraid one of your cans of milk may be left behind again, as it was the other day.'

'Yes', said Master Bull, 'Fayther said I be ollis to stop now and see it gu.'

'Very well, Master Bull', put in Tom Burley, 'but we can't have you in the way. Come and help move the cans, and then you can stand behind them on the platform and help in with them when the train comes.'

In this position I found Master Bull patiently waiting when I went out to see if the train was coming, after all the passengers were booked.

There were passengers of all descriptions, and amongst them were three young ladies walking together whose attention a very swell Commercial Traveller was evidently trying to attract.

He was a very smart man and very smartly dressed, took a first-class ticket, and travelled for nothing less than somebody's Blacking.

Suddenly he paused before the milk cans, and his sudden pause stopped the way for the young ladies, who were thus obliged to hear what followed.

Sticking an eye-glass into his right eye (probably a penny piece would have equally assisted his vision) he exclaimed in the most sonorous tone, '"Meilk," dear me, "Meilk"—Do you send meilk to London, Portaw?'

The porter thus addressed was Tom Burley, Porter No. 459, who had been talking to Master Bull about 20 eggs which he had promised to bring him for a shilling in the morning.

'Yes, sir,' said Tom Burley, touching his cap.

'Now what meilk is that?' continued the Commercial.

Tom answered, 'This is Bull's milk, sir.'

'You scoundrel!' said the Commercial.

'Haw, haw, haw,' said Master Bull, for he had positively seen the unhappy joke.

The Commercial took out his pencil and booked Tom Burley's number.

'I'll teach you to play your "Bull's milk" jokes on someone else,' said he, and so saying, strode into my office.

I had very great difficulty in keeping my countenance, for I heard what passed and only just popped in there to evade him, but I sent for Porter No. 459.

'Now, Sir', said the Commercial, 'I asked this porter, No. 459, what milk that was on the platform, and he coolly told me it was "Bull's Milk." I have travelled for some years, and I never met with such consummate impudence before. Not only that, there were ladies present, and I intend to write to the Directors about it. What is the name of that greenhorn yokel who stood next to him?'

'Begging your pardon', said Tom Burley, 'You asked whose milk it was?'

'I did not', interrupted the Commercial, 'and indeed, if I did, what excuse can that be for your impudence?'

'Why, *'tis* Bull's milk, sir, till he is paid for it.'

At this moment the Commercial bounced out of the office, and the train arriving, the cream of the joke had to be explained to him through the London Office, after he had written an elaborate report of our gross impudence and ignorance.

My wife's illness was productive of one good result, for through the Doctor she found out a very dear cousin, a farmer's wife living near, who subsequently took her for drives in her pony chaise, and who was godmother to another little boy who arrived in due course afterwards, and her dear little daughter was always coming to see us on her pony.

We spent many happy hours at her farm, and were very sorry to leave Fame on her account. The weekly cattle market was often productive as to practical jokes amongst the farmers and dealers, but somehow one of the neighbouring large villages always managed to produce a man who could, and did, acquit himself in such a way as to keep up the charter of possessing a bigger 'Silly' than any other place.

This charter was, however, nearly won by another village, which possessed a man who having bought a cow and a Welsh sheep, had tied the sheep to the cow's tail and started them on their homeward journey from Fame Market so secured.

The result of this was that the cow dragged the sheep to death, and had herself to be slaughtered to prevent her from dying as the result of the injury and fright.

Prophets said that the original village would not be long before it reclaimed its charter of having the biggest silly, and it was thus obtained.

Farmer Bark was opposed to fox hunting. He did everything in his power to annoy those who hunted, by putting wire fencing into his hedges, and applying for summonses against those who rode over his ground.

Finally they abandoned his farm and the covers on it, and Farmer Bark and the foxes were left to live undisturbed.

It does not take long for Master Reynard to discover an undisturbed home, and thus he took up his winter quarters with the farmer, whose young lambs and hen roost suffered in consequence.

The farmer was furious. All his neighbours laughed at him.

At last, one winter's morning, after it had been snowing all night, Farmer Bark awoke to find his hen roost robbed and many of his best fowls dead. It was a distressing picture. There was the fine old Dorking Tom dead, with his head off. There was no trace of the hen that was sitting on fifteen eggs and the eggs were cold, and only one of the seven young pullets was visible.

Everywhere were traces of blood, feathers, and foot marks on the white snow, and Farmer Bark shouldered his gun and vowed revenge. The severity of the weather prevented all hope of proceeding with any farming operations, and as the men came to work the farmer provided them with spades and pickaxes, and then they all started to follow Master Reynard's footsteps.

It was not a matter of any difficulty, for in addition to the track were stains of blood and an occasional feather dropped from the chickens which the fox had taken off with him. At last they came to the mouth of a drain, up which the rogue had undoubtedly taken his booty, for all trace ended there.

The farmer's little terrier went into the drain, and after a scuffle which was audible above ground, he came out yelping, with his nose severely bitten, and no inducement would persuade him to enter that drain again.

'Stop the drain up both ends', said the farmer, 'and begin opening of him in the middle.' Once open, the feathers again told the tale, and the position of Reynard was a matter of certainty.

An empty sack was placed like a rabbit net with its mouth open to the hole, in case the fox should attempt escape, and again they sounded on the top midway between the openings. This time the spade came through to Mr Reynard in such proximity that he thought it time to escape, and in so attempting he rushed into the open sack and was Farmer Bark's prisoner. Mr Bark took him home, slipped a cord round his neck, sack and all, and was about to hang him in his hen roost, when a party of young sportsmen who had been watching from the road, came and begged for the fox's life.

Farmer Bark was very wroth, but feeling his reputation would suffer, he at last consented to spare its life, though he was very loth to do so.

'He don't stop nowhere about here,' said Farmer Bark. 'Let them keep foxes as hunts. I'll send un to the Prince of Wales.'

It was owing to this resolution that I was very shortly afterwards favoured with a visit from Farmer Bark, who drove to the station in a gig, and walking into my office, pitched a dirty sack on to the counter with the poor fox's brush sticking out of it.

'Here, Young un', said he, 'Send this to the Prince of Wales.'

The first conclusion I arrived at was that the man had certainly gone mad, but seeing he was in earnest, and the poor fox's tail sticking out of the sack to which it was tied with string at the point where it protruded, I laughed aloud.

'You young fool, what are you laughing at?' said my visitor, 'Baint you a public servant; what do you mean by it?'

This insult stopped my laughing. I don't think anything else would have done it.

'You are not in earnest', I said.

'I tells you I wants that 'ere fox sent to the Prince of Wales, and it's more than you dares to refuse un, I tells ye.'

'But', I said 'you cannot compel us to take a thing that is not addressed. If you are going to be so strict with me I must tell you your duty.'

'Very well', said the farmer, ''Dress un.'

'No', I replied, 'that is no part of my duty, but here is pen, ink, and paper, write the address yourself.'

Farmer Bark took the pen, but he hesitated. At last he turned to me, and in a conciliatory tone enquired, 'What be I to write?'

I could scarcely be offended with him, so I replied, 'To His Royal Highness the Prince of Wales.' Then came the question as to where the fox would be acceptable. Sandringham was not purchased; a fox would not be wanted at Marlborough House, so there was nothing left but Windsor, and I said—'Windsor Castle, from T. Bark, of Addlepork.'

He wrote it, paid the carriage, and departed.

Reynard was rather offensive, so I placed him on the platform labelled 'Carriage paid to Windsor.' It was placed in the guard's compartment together with other parcels, and the effluvia was the first notice the guard had of it. So strong was it that the guard completed his journey to the next station with his head out of the window, when he handed it over to the next guard hoping he, too, would have a treat.

Three days elapsed, when in came Tom Burley with the identical sack, and fox's brush still untied, addressed to Farmer Bark. We opened the sack, in which were the remains of a rabbit, probably given to keep the fox alive, but his tail was very sore, and as it would take at least twenty-four hours for Farmer Bark to be advised by post and come in his gig, I determined not to allow it to remain in its court dress and train any longer, but to tie it up. Poor Dido's collar and chain were sent for for that purpose, and Dido's son, who had been returned to me by my uncle came with it from home. Then came the question, 'Who is going to put the collar round the fox's neck?'

No one volunteered, although all the men were present. I proposed that we should cast lots, and we did. It came to Tom Burley's lot. Foxy's head and neck were exposed, and whilst its attention was attracted in an opposite direction, Tom grabbed its neck and held it up whilst I put the collar round it.

What a beautiful set of teeth it had, and no wonder the little terrier was glad to escape from the drain. The office in the goods shed was the only place where we could tie it up to keep it under lock and key, and as there was no staple I thought it would be safe to tie the chain to the unused fire grate.

No sooner did I leave go of it than up the chimney it went to the extent of its chain, and there it remained until night, when it came down and ate a rabbit which we placed in readiness.

Dido's son usually accompanied me when I paid my daily visit to the fox. He was not an educated dog, but he was very intelligent and learnt to do many funny things, as if naturally. He pricked his ears considerably at the smell of the fox, and even ventured to sniff up the chimney, when down came the fox, and taking hold of his thigh, made its teeth meet. I could never get the dog into that office afterwards, for although the fox was not there, he would stand at the door and look towards the chimney as if to say, 'Once bit, twice shy. You don't catch me again!' A week elapsed and no Farmer Bark came for the fox, but the consequence was, that when the worthy farmer went to market there was an invisible cry, 'Who sent the fox to the Prince of Wales?'

The Earl of Flaxfield too, a tall, gaunt, red-haired earl who owned a pack of hounds, and whose lady was in favour at court,[1] actually condescended to enquire of me as to the facts of the case, and expressed a hope that the fox would not be 'chopped', but he did not leave anything towards its keep, and Mr Fox had run up a score of 8s for rabbits, besides back carriage.

There were, however, hunting men in the town, who made it a personal favour that I would try and save the fox, and although I hoped it would become my property, and had commenced to fit up a kennel for it at home, I was not anxious to see it handed over to the mercy of Farmer Bark.

Tom Burley said, 'What a lark 'twill be if old Farmer lets him go. The roughs and boys in the town are coming down when Old Bark comes for him, and if we don't have a spree my name's not Tom Burley.'

I laughed when I ought to have frowned, as I pictured the rage that Farmer Bark would be in if he lost his fox.

We had given up all hope of the fox being claimed, and had arranged for its removal to its new kennel, when Farmer Bark's gig was sighted.

'Here he comes', said Tom Burley, and away ran Tom into the town.

The farmer alighted, and, coming into the office, announced that he had come for his fox.

---

[1] The sixth Earl of Macclesfield; his wife was a Lady of the Bedchamber to the Princess of Wales.

I made out his bill, it was a heavy one, and his hand, which had been placed in his breeches for his leather purse, did not come out.

'Twelve shillings', said Farmer Bark, 'why I can get a dog kept a week for 6d.'

I produced receipts for rabbits, &c., and finally offered to pay for carriage and rabbits, and keep the fox myself, if he would allow me to do so.

'Never', said the farmer, 'he is my fox, and I'll have un', and so saying he paid the money.

By this time a goodly collection of roughs, boys, and dogs had assembled outside, and amongst them were some of the tradesmen who occasionally rode to hounds. I led the way to the goods office, and Tom Burley, after making sundry dumb motions, and stationing the crowd outside the goods shed in a particular position, followed.

'There it is, sir', said I, pointing to the chimney.

'Where' ? said the farmer.

'Why, up the chimney,' I replied.

'Then hand un down,' said Farmer Bark.

I told him that was no part of my duty, when Tom Burley took hold of the chain and pulled the fox down.

'Put him into this bag', said the farmer, producing one.

'Easier said than done', replied Tom.

The crowd outside began to hoot and exclaim 'Who sent the Fox to the Prince of Wales ?'

Farmer Bark was getting nervous. He was afraid to take hold of the fox himself, and he did not like to fork out a shilling for Tom Burley to place it in the bag, but the noise from the crowd decided him, and addressing Tom, he said, 'Here, young man is sixpence for you to untie him and put him in this bag.'

The fox had gone up the chimney again.

'I'll untie him,' said Tom, 'but I shan't take your money.'

Tom took hold of a potato fork that was in the office, and pulling Master Reynard down again, he shortened his distance by means of running this fork along the chain until he was completely pinned, and Tom seized him again by the back of his neck and unbuckled the collar.

'Now then', said Tom, 'hold the bag.'

Farmer Bark held the bag, but he was nervous, and exclaimed, 'Mind how you puts un in, young man !'

Tom said, 'Are you ready ?' and so saying dropped the fox, not into the bag but on to the bag, and away it went.

The farmer swore, the fox scampered, the crowd followed, and the tradesmen shouted, 'Gone away! gone away! gone away!' and the fox ran down the town pursued by all breeds of dogs and a crowd of men and boys.

An old black retriever chased it severely, but finally it got away from us all, and I confess I carefully avoided returning to the station until I had ascertained that Farmer Bark was absent.

Contrary to the usual habit of foxes this one could not have returned to its old quarters, for a few days later it was found, chased, and killed after a short run, and the ring mark round its bush proved it to be the same fox that was sent to the Prince of Wales.

Thus the joke outlived the fox, for they still say to Farmer Bark, 'Who sent the fox to the Prince of Wales?'

Mr Whirlpool took his annual holiday, and during his absence of three weeks Mr Levant came round the district once to see if we were all at our posts. He spent some hours at Fame, played a game at billiards with Mr Simens, at the Falcon, was flattered by the landlady in silk, and the young ladies played and sang to him. As he was leaving he became communicative, and between the whiffs of his pipe he delivered the following kind speech to me:

'Struggles, you told me you should like to get on the main line again. I have a vacancy at Byfield Station. If you like to apply for it I will consider your application. It will be a £10 increase for you.'

Of course I thanked him, and told him I would apply for it. The train by which he was going came up, and further discussion was impossible, but oh, what memories it had awakened.

# CHAPTER VIII

*Further Promotion—Webber, the Porter—Sawmouth, the Butcher—Out in the Snow—A Breakdown—Webber Shoots his own Cat—A Passenger Killed—Mr Dore—Charging a Station*

BYFIELD was my native place. For thirty years my father had farmed five hundred acres of land there. He had been churchwarden, overseer, and had moved in good society. I knew every man, aye, every boy, at Byfield, and my heart fluttered at the thought of returning to the place.

If I refused this promotion I might never get another chance, and why should I? and yet there was an inward feeling that made me dread returning to the place. However, I applied and was appointed.

It was no small matter to pack a house of furniture, a wife and child, three sacks of potatoes, two bushels of onions, four sacks of wheat, two sacks of barley, ten fowls, a cow and calf, three pigs, and ten sheep, but thus equipped I took possession of Byfield Station.[1]

My little dog was getting useful. He was a good dog to hunt, and possessed his father's nose. Not a yard of the ground for miles round but what I was familiar with it, and again I took to my gun, and to the snipes, hares, and moorhens.

Tom Burley wrote to say that he missed me, and that the man who succeeded me was above his post, and could not secure the confidence of anyone; but I found a substitute for Tom in one Webber, the parcels' porter, at Byfield, who, having been a gamekeeper's son, was naturally fond of sport.

Tom Burley was a young man, but Webber was a man in years. He had lifted me into the train at Byfield as a child, and he had been treated kindly by my father and mother. He did not forget it as some do, and although I knew little of him when I was a child, I soon found out that he

[1] 'Twyford is a station of some importance, being situated in a district that abounds more than most others with fine parks, country seats, and villas': G. Measom, *Official Illustrated Guide to the Great Western Railway*, 2nd ed. (1861), 63.

was one of the most trustworthy men that ever donned a suit of corduroys. Strictly attentive to his employers' business, civil and obliging to everybody, not hanging about for tips, and always at his post.

Webber was respected by all who came to the station, and thus he often came in for more than his share of work, for everybody asked for Webber.

He was not a good scholar, but he had nearly mastered the parcels accounts, which, strictly speaking, should be made up by the station master, and instead of handing over the books at the end of each month he made them up himself, and was very thankful for a little help to enable him to strike a balance, and which I cheerfully gave him.

How few unselfish men there are like Webber. I could have trusted my life in his hands, and it would have been safe. He was a 'perfect gentleman,' although a railway porter. In fact he was my factotum at Byfield.

In a very short space of time I found out that I should not be comfortable at Byfield.

The village gossip visited upon me the misfortunes of my father, and in consequence families with whom I had formerly associated were cold and distant.

I had been grossly insulted by a butcher, named Sawmouth, who had threatened to report me for not getting sufficient trucks on one occasion when no previous notice had been given.

My temper would have led me to retaliate at once, but Webber had fortunately stood in my way, and advised me to 'Bide my time.'

Mr Levant often favoured me with a visit; smoked a pipe in the little summer house on the bank, and gave the necessary orders.

One of these orders was to impress upon the staff the necessity of getting the trains away punctually, and another was, not to let people go without tickets.

'The Directors,' said Mr Levant, 'are now having a daily report of all passengers who travel without a ticket, and in every second case the station master at the station where they get in, will have to attend the Board, for travelling without tickets has been very much on the increase of late. And, with regard to the starting of trains punctually, the Directors have been going thoroughly into the matter, and they find that a minute lost at this station, and two minutes at that, all the way up, makes the train twenty, thirty, and forty minutes late arriving. So, Struggles, if you want to keep away from the Board, have your men drawn up in readiness to attend to the trains and get them away, but don't let the people go without tickets.'

Strange to relate, Mr Sawmouth was the first passenger who attempted to travel without a ticket. The train was three minutes late arriving, and just as it was about to start, Mr Sawmouth came rushing across the line and bundled into the train.

'Is it all right, sir?' said the guard.

'No,' I replied, 'come here, please.' I instructed him to ask Mr Sawmouth for his ticket.

Mr Sawmouth immediately replied, 'I suppose that cad clerk set you to do that. I have often travelled without a ticket, and I shall do so again. I defy you to remove me.'

Seeing me near to the carriage he called out, 'What does this mean, your setting this man to hunt me for a ticket? Some more of your dirty work I suppose?'

'It means, Mr Sawmouth, this,' said I, 'I have instructions not to let any one go without a ticket, and I shall not incur the risk of the Directors' displeasure on your behalf. If you don't come out at once I will myself remove you, as a dog would a rat.'

This might have been improper conduct on my part, or it might have served Mr Sawmouth right for insulting me before others as to my father's misfortunes, but I could not resist the spirit of retaliation, particularly as it came in the way of 'execution of duty,' and had not Mr Sawmouth thought proper to walk out of the carriage and slink off to the public house, I very much fear he would have suffered the uncomfortable ejection compared to the dog and rat business.

'I told you, sir,' said Webber, 'you would have the chance to put him straight, sir, and it will stop the rest of them, but I wish you had given him a good shaking and just knocked his head against the door by accident. How I should have enjoyed it, sir. He has been cocking about this village for some time but now he has got his master. Didn't he hook it out of the carriage when he saw you meant it. I'm as pleased as if anybody gave me a shilling, sir, and the best of it is, he aint got no pull.'

This meant that he had no ground for reporting me. This was the only passenger I ever detained for the want of a ticket.

It is too often the practice of station masters to exercise their petty authority in this particular matter, and in the case of Mr Sawmouth I was no better than others, but I have often witnessed the most cruel persecution of the public by their being detained for hours at a station unnecessarily, simply because they had not time to get a ticket, and although they were actually on the platform, money in hand, when the train came in, the station master, not knowing or caring for them, has said, 'You can't go by this train, you must wait and get a ticket for the next.'

Very true the Directors are naturally anxious to check travelling without tickets, and accordingly lay down certain rules and regulations to prevent it, but then it should be borne in mind that their object in so doing is to ensure the money for their passage coming into their coffers, and that money paid otherwise than by ticket does not always fall into the proper channel.

At the same time there is no reason why a passenger's money should not be handed to the guard of the train, and it would be less trouble to the station master to ascertain that the fare was paid, than it invariably is to listen to the bewailings of passengers thus left behind.

Most people travel from necessity. Probably a would-be passenger has received a telegram that his or her brother is just at the last and would like to see him or her. He may be going to the nearest town to get some article for which his men are waiting at home to complete some work. To stop a law suit, to attend a market, or summon a doctor, to catch a train on another line. In fact a thousand things, either of which would counterbalance the petty satisfaction of a station master being able to say before the public, 'No, you can't go without a ticket,' but I was not immaculate, so I will not lecture.

Now for a bitter winter night, such as many a railway man has passed out of doors, when the non-travelling public were at home, warm and comfortable.

It was snowing fearfully, with a piercing wind drifting the snow into the railway cuttings until it heaped up against the railway arches, which stopped its progress so as to make them appear to be the entrance to deep caves, and a few polar bears were only wanted to make the scene complete.

Where were the poor sheep and the little birds? Nothing to be seen of them; and indeed, where was the night mail? Nothing to be seen of it.

Tap, tap, tap, at the window of my bed room. It was with difficulty I opened it, and the snow fell in as I did so. It was the signalman. He had left his signals and his post, and ran to tell me that the night mail left Jam Junction at midnight, and the telegraph bell had sounded for it, but, although forty minutes had elapsed, it had not come in sight yet, and saying, 'you won't be long, sir, for I don't know what to do till you come,' he ran back to his signals, which were completely covered with snow, with only the smallest portion of the red light visible, which was soon out of sight altogether.

No second thought, but I struck a light, put on the thickest clothes at hand, thick boots, gaiters, and was off. I ran round the village and called the men up to come at once, and then made my way to the signalman's kennel, which by that time was covered with snow, and looked like part of a hollow tree with a man standing inside. It gave me a taste of the night, and I squeezed into the signal box to consult with the night signalman. There was barely room for both to stand.

'It come on so sudden,' said he, 'I don't expect the driver is provided with anything for snow, and it's quite uncertain where she is, but I expect she has broke down somewhere.'

Whoo-ho-hoo-hoo-ho-hoo-hoo-whoo-o-hooo. It was the brake whistle of the down express goods. She had caught sight of the danger signal, and came whoohooing into the station at the time I was talking, with an echo, which, but for the thickness of the falling snow would have awakened all the snoring villagers.

'What's up, mate?' said the driver to me, as I emerged from the policeman's kennel.

He had mistaken me for the signalman.

I explained to him, and he found out who I was, and said, 'What are you going to do, sir.'

'I am going to unhook your engine; leave your train here and run down to see what is the matter,' I replied.

The guard of this train waded through the snow to us as I was talking to the driver and his mate, who were by that time nearly covered with snow, for the engine had no roof to cover the driver.

Addressing the guard I told him he must go back a quarter of a mile behind his train and stand in the snow to warn the next coming train. He mumbled something about the train being inside the signals, his having one hundred and fifty miles to travel and no clothes to change, and enough to freeze a man.

I called him with me to the office, where I struck a light, booked his name, and wrote out an order something to this effect:—

'Guard Stokes,—Go back a quarter of a mile behind the signal with hand lamp and detonating signals to stop next train. Tell the next guard to go back and protect his train in the same manner, and to give the same order to the next guard, and so on.'

I took his receipt for the written order. The man looked at me as if he wished I was buried in the snow, and this unhappy railway servant walked off, to stand, may be an hour, in the snow, to get wet through, and probably catch his death cold, by afterwards drying his clothes before the engine fire, and by travelling one hundred and fifty miles, as if in a steaming flannel bag.

I made out the necessary *written* orders for blocking the line on which

I was going down, delivered a copy to the signalman, and accompanied by two or three porters, two brooms to tie on the engine to sweep the snow off the lines, and a few little requisites, jumped on the engine and went steadily down the line to see what had stopped the up mail.

'There she is,' said our driver as we turn a corner, 'and don't she look "rum."'

Indeed she did look 'rum,' as he called it, for one side of the train was sugared all over with snow, the windows of the carriages on that side were covered, and the passengers preferred to remain inside *to await their doom* to sitting in the snow. We pulled up, and our arrival was hailed with delight by the driver of the mail, his stoker, and the two guards, who were screwing about at the broken down engine. Some of the passengers were getting out.

'Keep your seats, there,' shouted the guard. 'There's deep man holes all along the line. I've just fell into one myself, and should have been smothered if my mate hadn't got a rope from the driver and pulled me out.'

This had the necessary effect on the passengers—for indeed the poor guard's appearance corroborated his testimony.

These 'man holes' are made to act as drains to the line, and I narrowly escaped walking into one myself, as they are open at the top.

The engine was immovable; she had broken down, and there was no help for it but to drag her into the next station, train and all, and change engines.

'Have you a man out behind?' I enquired.

'Oh, dear! no!' said the poor shivering fellow who had fallen in the man hole, and like a true Englishman, he forgot all his own troubles and rushed to his van, took his signals, and ran down the line to protect his train, but *only just in time*, for in a few minutes we hear another whoo-hoo-who-hoo-hoo, and the up goods is pulled up behind us, which would otherwise have pitched into the snow-bound train, no portion of which is visible behind.

'You won't report it, will you?' said the head guard, a good natured man, from whom I never received anything but kindness, 'the poor fellow fell into the man hole, and we were so "took up" with getting him out, that we forgot all about going back till you spoke, sir.'

How could I? Was not the poor man wet to the skin, shivering like a dog in December on a door step, and even then standing on the line in the snow?

'No.'

'Thank you, sir, you're a gentleman,' followed, and we consulted as to getting the train to my station.

'Try the tow-rope,' I said, for we had brought it.

We hooked it on to the stationary train and started. Pop! it went, and the rope barely missed the head of the guard who had been speaking, as it broke. It would surely have killed him on the spot had it struck him.

Nothing now to be done but to run back to Byfield on our engine, run down on the other line, and hook on to the broken-down train.

We had to go tender first, meeting the snow on our way back.

What a ride! What would I have given to have had Calcraft, the auditor; O'Reilly, the traffic superintendent; or one or two of the Directors with me on that occasion? Why, one month's salary!

We arrived at Byfield, placed the train belonging to my engine in the siding, allowed all down trains to proceed, and having written fresh orders for proceeding down the wrong line, we again reached the broken-down train. That time with a better result, for we dragged it into Byfield, shunted off the 'dead engine,' and sent the train on with a goods engine.

So far, so good, but the men *kicked* me for a little hot brandy and water, which I could not refuse them, but which, not being allowed by the Directors, I had to pay for out of my own pocket, and there was an engine to be telegraphed for to take on the goods train, a *full report* to be written out for Mr Levant, the District Superintendent, who will be up to enquire into the whole thing, possibly before I have changed my clothes and got a cup of hot coffee, and this was only one of about six break downs I had the good luck to conduct during my residence on the main line at Byfield.

I rather wished myself at Fame again, and indeed had it remained a terminus, I think I should have asked to go back.

Nothing like a terminus. If the trains don't come you can wait till they do, and you can always despatch your trains to time, because you are the starting point.

No train reports, no break downs, and no night work at a *small* terminus.

'Mr Struggles,' said Webber, the porter, rubbing his hands, 'can I run home after the cheap.'

Now I knew by this time, that when Webber rubbed his hands there was something in the wind, and, as that something in the wind was usually connected with a little bit of poaching, I looked enquiringly towards Webber who again rubbed his hands.

'Was it you who fired a gun off just now, Webber?' I enquired.

'Yes, sir,' said Webber, closing the door and talking confidentially. 'As I was having a wash, up stairs, I looked out of my window, and down at the bottom of my garden, just about thirty yards from hedge out in the field, there sat the daldest great hare as ever you set eyes on. I loads my old gun, crawls down on the snow, sticks my gun through the hedge, and lets fly. My eyes if she didn't jump, sir, a yard high and fell down dead. I took the gun indoors and was just going to fetch her when I saw Squire Parker coming along in his dog cart, so I thought I had better let her lie there till the cheap train had gone, and if you don't mind sir, I will just run home and take her indoors.'

'What will you take for her, Webber?' I enquired.

'Webber said he should not take anything of me, but finally I persuaded him to take half-a-crown for the hare, and provided him with a basket in which to bring her to the station.

Webber returned, but no basket. He avoided me and looked anything but pleasant.

At last I made bold to say, 'Where's my hare, Webber?'

Webber did not answer for some time, At last he mustered sufficient courage to do so, and told the tale as follows:

'I went home the back way, sir, thinking to pick her up and get over the hedge, but when I got to the place where I thought she was, there was the blood, and there was the fleck, but no hare. All round the place were cat tracks, so I followed them along into my pigstye, and there set my cat crope up in one corner all of a heap. It was she I had shot. I took her indoors and she lapped a little milk, but she is riddled all over with shots, and three have gone through her ears.'

So poor Webber had shot his cat for a hare.

I had unfortunately written to a friend to tell him I had sent him a hare, so I was in a fix.

I consulted with Webber. There had been another little fall of snow the next night, and it was still falling, and Webber suggested we should get on the top of the station, by means of a ladder, to see if he could point out a hare in either of the distant fields.

'There, sir,' said Webber, when we had mounted, 'do you see that brown spot? That's a hare,' and so it was, for he had scarcely spoken when the hare raised herself in form, and, shaking the snow from her back, settled herself down again.

The spot was marked, and shortly afterwards pussy had rolled over in the snow, a victim to my early practice with the fowling piece.

Webber described the recovery of his cat day by day. How the shots worked out of her, as he called it, and how gradually she shook off all symptoms of a full charge of shot at thirty yards distance, which would certainly have killed a hare.

Much dissatisfaction was created by the promotion of Mr Badger to be station master at Jam Junction, where he received a salary of £200 per annum, and in which capacity he never lost an opportunity of writing in a dictatorial tone to myself and to other neighbouring station masters, all of whom had double his experience, but who lacked a brother as assistant secretary to the Board of Directors.

Byfield Station was not only on the main line, but it also boasted of being the Junction for the neighbouring town of Benley,[1] so that many passengers changed at Byfield, and the porters called out 'Byfield! change here for Benley.' It was one of my constant directions to the men to call out loudly and distinctly, and I flatter myself it was done.

A train had pulled up, and had started again, when I saw the door open of the last carriage, and a man get out with a large hamper. The train had started at a good pace, and he fell on to the platform, having hold of the hamper. Immediately followed a stout woman, his mother; but she had no hamper. She stepped out of the train, staggered, and fell behind the carriage in which she had been riding on to the line, and a truck passed over her. A faint 'Oh!' was all that we heard from her. We lifted her on to a four-wheel trolley, and, placing a cushion under her head, we drew her to the hotel, where she was carefully tended, but she never spoke again.

They were country people, who rarely travelled, and the son said that at Jam Junction he was told that Benley was the second station, and that therefore he concluded he had not to change at Byfield, but having heard the porters call out so distinctly 'Byfield! change here for Benley,' he inquired of a fellow-passenger, after the train had started, as to whether he was right. 'You ought to have changed here,' said the fellow passenger, and so we got out as quick as we could. 'I got out first, to help mother,' said the man, 'but I fell down with the hamper.' No doubt, the hamper saved his life. The inquest took place in due course, and I was severely questioned as the propriety of starting the trains so rapidly, but as witnesses attended to say that sufficient time was allowed for them to alight, the Coroner and the Jury exonerated us from all blame, and the son went on his journey with his poor dead mother.

Near to Byfield lived a Mr Boldway, brother to Captain Boldway, the Director.[2] He was as unlike his brother as it was possible for him to be; for, whilst the Captain (Captain Tom, as he called him) was active, energetic, and commanding, Mr Boldway was quiet, retiring, and unassuming. I did not know the interest this family had in the Great Smash Railway; but it seemed that my manner of conducting the business of the station induced them to speak of me in favourable terms to the Captain, who,

---

[1] Henley.

[2] Capt. Bulkeley.

in common with other directors, selected me for a post of great responsibility later on. The Boldways were descended from people of great distinction, and, although the porters would have flown to wait on them at the mention of the Captain's name, they never traded on his position, but accepted little civilities in the kindest possible manner, so that it was a pleasure to do anything for them.

Although the duties of station-masters on each line of railway are precisely the same, and framed to agree with that mighty divider, the Railway Clearing House—which at this moment employs an unlimited number of clerks, to divide and arrange certain small matters for railway companies, which they cannot well arrange without an agreed tribunal of some sort—it is most amusing to notice the extraordinary difference, in bodily garb and appearance, of the railway companies' representatives who play the part of station masters.

For instance, if you take a ride by a down train on a certain railway, at stop No. 1 you would see a kind of inspector in the company's best livery appear. His buttons shine and his face shines, and being devoid of whisker and possessed of a very fat face and plump body, he presents altogether the appearance of a living sausage dressed in buttons, and with two smaller sausages as arms.

Then at stop No. 2, a very sad, shabby man appears in plain clothes, and wearing the company's official cap. This man impresses you with the immediate conviction that he has seen better days, and as the train starts he walks sadly back to his office without a smile.

At No. 3 station, a fat porter, dressed in corduroy tights, appears as station-master, evidently on excellent terms with himself and the guard, and he rides a little way on the step, and talks to that official, after he has started your train, dropping off with a scientific plump on to his heel, when he thinks the train is going too fast for him to venture further.

Then at No. 4, a boy-clerk station master emerges from the office, very small and very thin, and wearing an official cap, under which he appears to walk like a young crab in a whelk shell.

At No. 5, a tall, seasoned station master stalks out, with a black beard to his waist, and a profusion of whisker. He is miserably thin, very shabby, and but for the official cap you might mistake him for a hair-dresser's living advertisement.

Then at No. 6 stop, a jolly, nice looking young man appears as station master, with a smile and a joke for everyone, and you wonder how long he will remain at that station, and how the company happened to possess such a man.

Perhaps at No. 7 station you might see a man very like my old friend, Mr Mulberry, before described.

At any rate, they would form a very odd lot if they were wanted for military service—as in Germany—and I don't think Mr Mulberry would ever drill straight.

So it is, and so it was, and I don't think two station masters were ever more unlike each other than myself and Mr Dore, who was station master at Benley. *He was a bashful man;* and, not only that, he was a nervous man, and he quite trembled in the presence of ladies. He was not unlike my fellow-clerk at Puzzle Junction (Mr Hensler), but instead of *brooding* over his troubles, he soliloquized.

His accounts were in a dreadful state of confusion, and he had three drawers of unaswered letters. The fatal system of correction, still adopted by railway managers, had got fairly hold of him, and poor Dore was vainly endeavouring, like a mouse in a pail of water, to keep afloat. Mr Fretsum not only bullied because his monthly accounts were not in, but he demanded a written explanation in each case as to why about forty different accounts were not sent in. The District Goods Manager, whose cognomen was 'Little Tommy,' was down upon Dore to the extent of no less than 250 letters about the outstandings, and other matters to which he required replies; and Mr Calcraft spent two whole days there to hinder poor Dore, and to see if he could find him 'short in his cash.' But no; Dore was an honest and upright man, and his only fault was, that nature had evidently intended him for a girl, and he lacked the necessary energy and combative power to swim out of his difficulties. Very few men ever do swim out of a similar dilemma, because the system, you will see, heaps up the agony and drowns the mouse.

Poor Dore told me all his troubles, and occasionally came to consult with me as to matters of difficulty. He would walk to the end of the railway platform, select some rural picture, and look up to the heavens and sigh, perhaps saying—'Do you see that man working there, Mr Struggles? He is happy, but I am not happy. I wish I had your happy disposition. I couldn't take charge of this main-line station if you gave me all the world.'

Mr Levant was annoyed at the repeated complaints as to Dore's deficiency, and, wishing one day to go to Benley to look him up, he inquired of me if there was any chance of his finding a train other than the regular one, to enable him to catch a certain train home. There was an empty engine coming up, and I told him of it.

'Come down, Struggles,' said Mr Levant, 'and just take a copy of his station account. I haven't patience with the man.'

The meeting was a very stormy one, and Mr Levant left in anything but a good temper, together with myself, on the engine. The engine-driver was out of humour at having to wait for us. I amused myself by witnessing the unconcern which hares, rabbits, pheasants, partridges, and moorhens exhibited at our passage. The fiery monsters never injure them—they have no fear; whereas the presence of a little weazel would fill them with consternation.

Byfield Station was approached by a rather steep gradient, and as we neared it the goods train by which Mr Levant wished to go pulled up.

'What do you want to shut off steam for?' said Mr Levant to our driver. 'Do you want me to miss that train?'

'You can have more steam if you like,' growled the driver, and he put on a sufficient quantity to immediately convince me that he would not be able to pull up before he came to the horse-box, which stood in front of us at the dead end. It was further evident to your humble servant that 'a cannon' was unavoidable, and, not wishing to sit on the cue whilst the engine played bagatelle with the horse-box and the station, Ernest Struggles descended to the step of the engine on the off side, and dropped on to the line safely. Mr Levant, too, jumped from the left side of the engine on to the platform, but alighting like a frog dropped from an eminence, he was somewhat disarranged. The driver and his mate sat their old horse manfully, which, having cannoned the horse-box, drove it with one jump into the pocket of the first-class waiting-room through the window, and then re-charging, the engine took the corner of the station, a stone building, and misplaced a large portion of the masonry.

Fortunately, no old ladies were in the waiting-room to receive the horse-box, and Mr Levant was the only person upset. It was some time before his breath returned sufficiently for him to light his pipe, and it was some weeks before he was able to leave his house and the Accidental Society, and by that time I had bid good-bye to his district, and left the most manly and best superintendent I ever had the good luck to serve under.

## CHAPTER IX

*Further Promotion—Bittern and its Surroundings—Mr Sprigalilly—Mr McLion—A Smash—Up before the Board—The Long and Narrow Railway—Joe War in trouble—Suicide of Webber*

BITTERN[1] Station became vacant. I applied for it, and obtained the appointment. It was 150 miles from Byfield, and in the very centre of the coal and iron district.

In addition to a salary of £90 per annum, a house on the top of the station (which was approached by a staircase with 40 steps), together with coal and stores, was provided. By stores was meant brushes, brooms, mats, and soap; no food or raiment. I sold cow, sheep, and pigs, save one black sow, and removed to Bittern Station, arriving there at night.

The sight was lovely, for the burning cinder mounds and flaming iron works illumined the whole country for miles round with different hues and flames.

To one who has not travelled through that part, it would be a most interesting tour at night, but let such traveller be 50 miles away in the morning; for of all the awful places by day, it is the worst.

It is man's habitation apart from the beauties of nature, of which there is not a trace.

No trees or grass to be seen; no gardens; no birds, save sparrows, black as ink; very little attempt at art in the building of the houses; the children dirty beyond extreme; black mud, or black ash-dust everywhere; the people ill clad, and dirty, by reason of their occupation; the fowls even have no gloss on their dirty feathers; the dogs dirty, and dirty white pigs everywhere. Such was Bittern. The only time I saw it look at all pleasing was when a deep fall of snow had mantled it with a clean robe.

The people, too, were something quite new to me, and to give you an idea of their intellectual state, I may mention that, after the capture of Sebastopol, two colliers met at Bittern Station, and the following dialogue was overheard:—

[1] Bilston, Staffs.

*No.* 1—'They've took that Sebastopool, Bill.'

*No.* 2—'Have they? I hope they'll hang him.'

*No.* 1—'Hauld th' noise, Bill. Tyen a mon; 'tis a place.'

But I must leave the people for a little while, and trouble you to follow me round to my new duties. I was a double station master at Bittern Station —that is to say, I had two stations to manage, and these stations were three quarters of a mile distant, running parallel with each other. They had formerly been opposition lines, but the smaller one had been bought up by the Great Smash, after the company had run down its rival.[1]

There were some ridiculous facts in connection with the cheap fares and concessions, of which the public had the benefit during the running-down process; in fact, they almost took the people for nothing, and gave them something to drink. But that was all over before my arrival; and with a staff of six clerks, 35 men, and 12 horses, I reigned supreme over both stations.

These 12 horses were in constant work, taking goods out and bringing iron in, and it was with some satisfaction that I eyed them with a determination soon to have their coats a little more glossy, and their harness brightened up, for they were fine, powerful animals.

My father had always kept 12 horses to plough at our old farm, and the presence of these went part of the way to reconcile me to my isolated position.

There was a little hen-house adjoining the stable, where I could keep a few fowls, which would live on the waste corn from the stable; and a place for my black pig.

The clerks were all respectable young men, but the work was as much as they could possibly get through, for 80 of the iron-masters and tradesmen were allowed a monthly ledger account, which entailed a great deal of work.

The telegraphic instrument was in the booking-office, where one clerk only was engaged.

It was a double-needle instrument, and no one, save myself, could work it. My attention was fully taken up by starting trains, opening quite 300 business letters daily, collecting 80 ledger accounts monthly, canvassing for traffic in opposition to the Long and Narrow Railway,[2] checking and

---

[1] The two stations at Bilston came to be known as 'Bilston and Ettingshall', on the G.W. line from Birmingham to Wolverhampton, and 'Bilston and Deepfields' on the Wolverhampton–Dudley line. The former line had originally been promoted by the Birmingham Wolverhampton & Dudley Railway, which was bought by the Great Western in 1850.

[2] The London & North Western Railway.

balancing all accounts, and reading and signing a huge heap of letters daily that were written in answer to those received, and on the general business of the station. I therefore wrote to Mr Sprigalilly, the telegraph superintendent, to inform him there was no one to watch this instrument.

Mr Sprigalilly was a gentleman of great pretensions. I think his mother had kept a fried fish shop, and sold gingerbeer and tripe; but Mr Sprigalilly had fortunately been one of the earliest engaged as a telegraph boy, and had risen to be manager of the department.

To see Mr Sprigalilly from behind was a treat. The cut of his coat was perfection (nothing less than Poole), and his peg-top trousers had been pressed, and came out as if new. I expect he had two pairs—one in the press and the other in wear. Then his boots were of patent leather, his hat quite newly ironed, and such a lovely lavender silk necktie, with lavender gloves to match; but when Mr Sprigalilly turned round he most unfortunately revealed a red-spotted face in contrast with a white waistcoat, which, together with carroty whiskers and moustache, a very red nose and blear eyes, told unmistakeable tales of port wine, bottled stout, *or* erysipelas.

He replied to two of my communications briefly as follows:—

Dear Sir,

Yours *re* instrument at Bittern has attention.

Yours truly,

To Mr Struggles. C. E. Sprigalilly.

Some months elapsed, and I wrote again, when he replied that time by writing across the back of my letter himself:—

Dear Sir,

In answer to this matter, we contemplate changing the instrument from a double needle to a single needle one, and under these circumstances it would be waste of time to teach your people the working of the double needle, which is entirely different. The matter must therefore rest until then.

Yours truly,

To Mr Struggles. C. E. Sprigalilly.

I have troubled you with these letters because they will become very important documents later on.

Mr Justice, the District Passenger Superintendent,[1] was a kind old

[1] G. N. Tyrrell, Superintendent of the Northern Division, Great Western Railway, 1860–64; Superintendent of the Line 1864–88.

gentleman, but he was entirely over-ruled by the District Goods Manager, Mr McLion, a Scotchman.[1]

Up to this time the directors of the Great Smash Railway had overlooked all claims on the part of goods traffic on this line. Goods trains were shunted for days together to make room for passenger trains, and Mr O'Reilly, the traffic superintendent, who knew nothing about the working of goods traffic, was continually waging war with Mr McLion, with respect to the attempts of the latter to bring the value of goods traffic prominently before the directors.

At this very time Mr McLion had hopes of success. He was a man of good appearance, fawned to those over him, and oppressed those under him. Englishmen cannot cringe to Scotchmen, although Scotchmen may be put in authority over them; but as many Scotchmen originally made their way in England by cringing to Englishmen, they expect the submission from others which they have themselves offered at the shrine of fame. They don't get it, and they don't agree. This was my position with Mr McLion from my very first interview, and it never changed. He went through the list of outstanding accounts of all stations monthly, for which purpose the station-agents had to attend his office at Stork,[2] and explain each item in detail. Bitter were his remarks, bitter was his demeanour, and bitter is my remembrance of those monthly meetings. He would take an outstanding item, say—'Jones, 9d. Now then, Mr Struggles, why is this amount outstanding? Where are the papers?' I hand in copies of twenty letters posted to Jones about this 9d, demanding payment (don't lose sight of the fact that the stamps cost 1s 8d), to none of which I have received a reply.

'Have you seen Jones?'

'Yes, sir.'

'What does he say?'

'Mr Jones says that when he gave a cheque for his December account, and which I find amounted to £33 8s 9d, he wrote it short 9d as he never pays coppers to anyone else with whom he deals; but that if we are so particular about 9d, there is an old claim of £3, which he made some twelve months since, for some broken "sad irons,"[3] for which he must press. Don't you think, sir, we had better drop the 9d and then he won't trouble about the claim?'

[1] James Grierson, afterwards (1865) General Manager of the Great Western Railway.

[2] Wolverhampton.

[3] Flat smoothing irons.

Mr McLion looked at me, compressed his lips, turned up his nose, and scowled at me as if I was a dog. He then proceeded to say—

'Now, then, see Jones to-morrow; get particulars of his claim, fill in all particulars, such as reference to entry, copy of invoice, who brought the goods to the station, attach the carman's *written* statement as to condition of goods, turn up the consignment note to see if your checker made any remark as to condition. Telegraph receiving station to see consignee, and wire you condition received in, and let me have a full report from yourself on foolscap before I leave the office to-morrow, together with the proper claim report form.'

Then Mr McLion would pass on: I was going to say to the next cage, but I mean to the next item, and deal with that after the same style. I never got off under two hours of standing before this slave-driver, and, when I did get off, I had enough unpleasant work looked up for the next month.

If Williams did not pay his account by Friday, I was to seize his goods, and lock them up.

If Johnson did not remove his coal, I was to sell it, and stick to it all for demurrage and siding charges, and so on.

Mr McLion's treatment to the customers was precisely the same; in fact, everybody shrunk within himself as his name was mentioned, excepting just a favoured few—wealthy traders—to whom he paid his obeisance, taking care to be seen with them as often as possible on the Exchange and in public.

I was naturally anxious to have done with these monthly ordeals, or at any rate to shorten them by clearing up and clearing off the items; I gave the greater part of my attention to them.

Many good customers were offended by the annoyance to which they were subjected, and some removed their traffic to the Long and Narrow Railway. I soon found it necessary to look up new customers, in order to keep up my returns, and amongst these was a large firm of bedstead-makers, named Lerry & Sons,[1] whose carriage was very considerable, and of which we had not one iota.

Now, I made up my mind that I would have part of these people's carriage, or know the reason why. Calling at the manager's office, my first attempt was to see him, and ask for a share of the traffic.

He received me kindly, but stated that the firm had a decided preference for the Long and Narrow Railway Company, and that the matter did not

---

[1] Thomas Perry & Co, Highfields, Bilston.

rest with him. One by one, at different times, I saw the members of that firm individually, and pressed for part of their traffic, but with no better result, until at last I felt convinced that there must be some reason, other than a personal one, for this reluctance to trade with us.

The Long and Narrow Railway paid their station-agent better than the Great Smash Company, were not so narrow in their allowances for trifling expenditure to the foremen of works, and instead of moving their station-agents before they would grant them a rise of salary, they gave them occasional rises, and kept them for years in one town, knowing that a man who was conversant with the peculiarities of the traders and of the traffic must have an advantage over a stranger.

The Long and Narrow Company's station-agent had been five years at Bittern. He knew everybody; and when he called to canvass for the traffic he was empowered to give the foreman of the works 1s to drink his health. I was not allowed to do this.

At the same time the Long and Narrow Railway Company and the Great Smash Company had agreed to charge equal rates for carriage of goods to London, and to other towns where both had a station.

If I wanted to know anything particular about custom of the trade in that district, I usually inquired of some of the chief traders. Amongst these were Messrs. Bolter Brothers & Co., and one or other of these people (for there were two brothers and a son) was sure to be at the station in the course of the day.

Bolter Brothers & Co. had been bankrupts no less than seven times, but as they had made money by failing each time they were then well to do—drove a smart horse and dog-cart, dealt largely in iron, and having money, they were quite looked up to. If, on the other hand, they had not made money by failing, and had given everything up to their creditors, they would have been treated as fools, and spoken of accordingly.

I made known my difficulty as to Lerry & Son's traffic to Messrs. Bolter Brothers & Co. Mr Bolter, sen., scratched his head, and answered as follows:—'You think as I can help ye, dun yaw? Well, it so happens that aw've got a sister's daughter what's married to a yoing mon as is in the works at Lerry & Co.'s, and her's a comin' to our place to-night, and her husband's a comin' too, and we're going to have a bit of supper. Aw think as we've got a sooking pig, and if yaw likes to come up aw'l tell him to give ye the "straight tip" about it. Bring the missus wi' ye.'

Accordingly I went to Mr Bolter's house to supper, and took 'the missus' with me. The house was furnished most elaborately. Everything was very massive and heavy; but the heaviest articles were two immense oil paintings of Mr and Mrs Bolter, with enormous gilt frames, and which nearly covered one wall of the room.

The paintings themselves were miserable attempts at art; but the painter had carefully copied the striking imperfections of both. There was no mistaking them.

The sucking-pig, stuffed with sage and onions, came on the table at one end, an immense dish of tripe at the other end, surrounded with boiled leeks.

'That theire sooking pig will never sook his mother again,' said Mr Bolter.

'Bring in the champagne, Trifosa.' Mrs Bolter, whose Christian name was Trifosa, produced four bottles of champagne, and our hearts began to open.

'This yoing mon's leaving Lerry & Son's next week,' said Mr Bolter, 'so if yow want to know anything yow must be quick about it. He is going to open a liquor-shop next week. But what is Mr McLion going to make him a present of if he gives you the straight tip?'

I guaranteed a sovereign, was thereupon promised a sight of the Long and Narrow Railway Company's monthly account, on the following day, during the clerks' dinner hour. Mr Bolter dilated on the experience of life, and wound up the evening by strongly advising me never to go in for anything less than a 'big thing,' but to mind that in all my transactions through life I always left a 9-inch hole for a 7-inch man, or, in other words, room to back out of a difficulty.

At dinner time on the morrow I presented my sovereign and myself at Messrs. Lerry & Son's office, was shown the Long and Narrow Railway Company's accounts, and finally allowed to pocket one of them to copy, in which almost every article was charged at a less rate than the one mutually agreed upon by the two companies, thus giving the Long and Narrow Company an unfair advantage over the Great Smash. I copied the account and returned it.

Mr McLion lived at Bass Station, but his offices being at Stork, he necessarily passed Bittern Station on his way to business, and so did Mr Justice, the passenger superintendent.

These gentlemen were in receipt of £500 per annum each, together with first-class season tickets to travel with, and an allowance for daily expenses incurred.

They usually travelled in the same carriage, and, of course, we were on the look out for the train by which they were expected to pass, as instructions of some kind would be forthcoming from one or from both of them.

It was a very foggy morning when, as usual, Mr McLion put his head out of a first-class carriage, and said to a porter, 'Where's Struggles?' The porter called me, and Mr McLion told me to come to Stork by the next train, as he wanted to see me particularly. I remonstrated with him, as I had made several appointments at the station; further, I told him that it was very foggy, and scarcely safe for me to leave the station.

Mr McLion made no observation in reply to my remonstrances, but merely threw himself back in his seat, and addressing Mr Justicc, who sat opposite to him, he said, 'Is he to come or not?' Mr Justice said, 'I suppose so, if you want him;' and there the matter ended, for I started the train. By the next one I repaired to Stork, and was informed by a small office boy that Mr McLion was waiting for me.

'Struggles,' said Mr McLion, 'I went through the returns of your station yesterday, and find that there is a falling off in the traffic. If you cannot account for it satisfactorily, I shall apply to the directors for your immediate removal from my district. I will not have a man near me who cannot keep the traffic up.'

'Well, sir,' said I, 'you know I have been busy with the outstandings, and that the pressure I have to put on the customers to collect them offends people. Besides, the Long and Narrow Company's agent is allowed to tip the foremen at the works. The Long and Narrow Company do not charge demurrage, and that affair of our selling Johnson's coal, to pay siding charges, the other day, is talked about.'

'Do you think I am a child!' said Mr McLion. 'Have you no other excuse?'

'Yes,' I said. 'The Long and Narrow Company do not charge the same rates as we do.'

'The Long and Narrow Company,' interrupted Mr McLion, 'no more dare charge different rates than I dare keep you to lose all the traffic.'

'But they do so, sir,' and producing a copy of their account with Lerry & Sons, I handed it to Mr McLion, who said—'What is this?' I explained the nature of the document, and Mr McLion eyed me with a keen, doubtful look, and was about to reply, when a railway policeman rushed into the room to inquire if Mr Struggles was there. The man did not know me, but I made myself known to him, and he very speedily informed me that there had been a most awful smash at Bittern Station;[1] that the up express train had pitched into the goods train, which she failed to notice by reason of the fog; and, further, that one of the Directors (the Captain) was in the train. I did not stay to say more to Mr McLion, but I very soon joined the 'breakdown gang,' who had been summoned to go with their van, which is

---

[1] See p. vi, n.2.

especially fitted and filled with screw-jacks, tools, and requisites, and assist with the wreck of the two trains. There were several trucks thrown off the line, and the passenger engine was off too. The train was going a good pace when she suddenly came upon the goods train, which was in the act of being shunted into the siding at the station beyond Bittern. She smashed the guard's van after the fashion in which you could smash a hat box with your foot; and inside it was the unfortunate guard, whose death must have been instantaneous.

Miraculous to state, beyond bleeding of noses, by people's heads being knocked together, and bruises to people who had been thrown across the carriages, no one was seriously injured, and the Captain (the Director) was going about like a captured wasp in a wine glass. Didn't he sting, too! Those who predict that railway accidents will never cease until so many railway directors have been killed in one, should have been present at this little entertainment. So frightened were the men at the Captain, his orders and his commands, that the dead body of their poor mate lay on the railway bank unheeded. At last, directing Mr Justice to bring all concerned 'up before the Board' on the following Board-day, the Captain took his departure, and reserved all further wrath for that occasion.

It was a great day that Board-day, and the Captain, with sundry pieces of sticking plaister on his face, sat holding his own inquest over his own body. The Great Smash Company's rule book was placed before the chairman of the directors, and one by one we were all examined as to the cause of this sad accident. There was very little mention about the guard who was killed. No inquiry as to whether he had a family, or whether they were in great distress or in want; but there was constant reference to the Captain, who sat there the living hero of the occasion. At last, my turn came, and the old fat doorkeeper at the board-room called out, 'Mr Struggles, you are wanted.' In another minute I was before the Board, and again 'the picture' smiled on me.

'Mr Struggles,' said the Captain, 'where were you when this accident happened?'

'I was at Stork, sir.'

'What did you do there?'

'I went to see Mr McLion.'

'What! To see Mr McLion! Surely you could have seen him at any time. At what time did you go?'

'At 9.30, sir.'

'Was it foggy then?'

'Yes, sir.'

'How long have you been in our service?'

'Seven years, sir.'

'And do you mean to say that you have been for seven years in the service of this company, and don't know that it is advisable on a foggy day to stop and look after your trains, in preference to any other business?'

Now, here was a fix. It was always the case, and I suppose it always will be so, than when an accident happens the station master cannot escape, because if he is absent he ought to be present; then again, if he be present he ought to prevent the accident; but I knew very well that my answer to this question must reflect very strongly upon Mr Justice, so I was silent.

'Don't you hear what I say, sir,' said the Captain, standing up and facing me with his black plaister patches.

'Yes, sir,' I replied.

'Then why on earth don't you answer!'

I saw Mr Justice look at Mr McLion, who was sitting at the Board table with him, but Mr McLion did not move a muscle. I verily believe that if I had been going to be hanged, Mr McLion would not have spoken to save me.

'Disgraceful conduct,' remarked the deputy chairman, Mr Alexander Stone.[1] 'I think we should dismiss Struggles without further inquiry. I was very nearly coming up by that train myself.'

To my infinite relief, Mr Justice rose and explained to the directors that I had hesitated to leave my station that morning, but that Mr McLion had particularly required my attendance at Stork, and that he had sanctioned my going.

'Is that a fact, Mr McLion?' said the Captain.

Mr McLion rose, and addressed the directors as follows:—

'Gentlemen,—If you will kindly waive this question for a few minutes, I will presently explain to you my motive for so particularly requiring the attendance of Struggles at my office on that morning, and I have to bring before your notice matters of the most vital importance in connection with the Long and Narrow Railway Company, and which will absorb too much interest to allow me judiciously to mention them just now in connection with this very sad calamity, and as my suspicions could not be confirmed without the personal testimony of Struggles, I was naturally anxious to take his evidence; but I may say at the time when Mr Justice sanctioned his coming to Stork, there was every appearance of the fog clearing off.'

[1] (Sir) Charles Alexander Wood, Deputy Chairman, Great Western Railway, 1865–89.

The crafty Scotchman was undoubtedly going to take the whole of the credit of obtaining the information about the Long and Narrow Railway Company's undercharges to himself, and, not content with that, he sought to clear Mr Justice, and to saddle me with the responsibility of leaving the station during the fog. Naturally impulsive and hasty, I was about to unmask the cunning Scot, but the moment I spoke, Mr Alexander Stone said—

'Will you wait until you are spoken to, sir. You lacked common perception and now you are going to add impudence to ignorance.'

The Captain continued the inquiry.

'We will see Mr Justice and Mr McLion, Mr Struggles, with reference to your leaving your station; but as it appears you are in the habit of leaving to collect accounts and to canvass for traffic, I now wish to know how it is that you have not made proper arrangements for the working of the station during your absence. Who did you leave in charge?'

'The booking-clerk, Mr Shakespear.'

'How long has Mr Shakespear been in the service?'

'Six months, sir.'

'Is Mr Shakespear here?'

'Yes, sir.'

Mr Shakespear was called in, and placed beside me—not in the dock, but at the end of the table facing the picture and the Captain.

'Now, Mr Byron, I mean Mr Shakespear,' said the Captain—and for the first time the directors, save and except Mr Alexander Stone, who stamped his foot, smiled—'you were in charge of Bittern Station when the accident happened?'

'Yes, sir.'

'What did Mr Struggles tell you when he left?'

'He told me, sir, that I was to keep a good look out, and that I had better not go to dinner.'

'And did you keep a look out?'

'Yes, sir.'

'Did you not know when the express train was due to pass Bittern?'

'Yes, sir.'

'Then why on earth did you start the goods train?'

'Because she had done her work, sir.'

'But surely you knew there was barely time for the train to get to the next station, and that in foggy weather no goods train is allowed to go on unless she has 15 minutes start of a passenger train?'

'No, sir.'

'Have you no rule book?'

'Yes, sir.'

'Then have you not studied it?'

'I have read half of it, sir.'

Addressing Mr Justice, the Captain inquired what salary Mr Shakespear was getting. He was informed £50 per annum.

A general murmur commenced amongst the directors. They had secured a culprit, and they wanted to consult as to what to do with him. We were ordered to leave the room.

When we were recalled, Mr Alexander Stone addressed Mr Shakespear as follows:—

'The directors have carefully considered the case against you, Mr Shakespear, and they think that you have been most negligent in not studying your rule book. To imagine that any man can remain six months in the service of a railway company, without making himself master of 120 pages of rules, is to them a thing unparalleled, and proves that you are no longer worthy of their confidence. That, however, is a matter of little importance connected with the fact that you did not even trouble to telegraph the departure of the trains to the next station. We have decided to dismiss you from the service.'

'But, gentlemen,' I said, 'Mr Shakespear does not understand the telegraph.'

'Not understand it!' said Mr Stone. 'Then why did you not teach him?'

'I beg pardon, sir, but I have no time to teach telegraph at Bittern. I wrote to Mr Sprigalilly, and told him there was no one who understood the telegraph in my absence, and asked him to send someone to teach Mr Shakespear.'

Mr Sprigalilly rose in all his splendour, not like the lily which Solomon wrote about, for indeed the white waistcoat was the only thing approaching it, but like a groggy prevaricator, which he proved himself—for he declared that I had never written him on the subject.

Upon the booking-clerk's incompetency, and the lack of the use of the telegraph, thus turned the whole accident. The booking-clerk was to remain suspended, and I was to come up on the following Board-day with evidence of my having communicated with Mr Sprigalilly; and the first ordeal was over.

As I left the room, the Captain called out to me, 'You recollect, Struggles, you have to prove that you wrote to Mr Sprigalilly, and received an answer to your letter.'

Although the journey was 180 miles, Mr Sprigalilly presented himself at Bittern Station in company with Mr Justice the next morning. He was dressed to death, as usual—had on lemon-coloured kid gloves. He walked into my office as if he was the owner of the whole railway, and placing his back to the fire, and leaning against the mantelpiece, said—

'You made a pretty statement before the directors, Struggles; I have come to see what letters you have of mine.'

Now, had he been alone, I think it just possible that I might have opened the office door and requested him to leave, but Mr Justice was with him, and he followed up Mr Sprigalilly's remarks by adding—'Yes, you had better turn the letters up, Mr Struggles. I will wait.'

As I had great respect for Mr Justice, I curbed my feelings, and, diving into my cupboard, I brought out an armful of headed correspondence, and commenced to search.

Mr Sprigalilly took off his gloves, and searched too. He searched in earnest, but I searched for fun, for I knew that all the letters I had brought out had reference to goods matters only, and that the passenger and telegraph letters were locked in a drawer below.

Had Mr Sprigalilly said, 'Struggles, if you really have any letters from me, I shall take it as a favour your sending me copies of them,' he would have had them; but when he sought to bully me, he roused a feeling which was not likely to assist him in his mission.

Two hours of this work settled him, and, having told Mr Justice that the thing was all a 'myth,' he expressed his readiness to return with him to Bass Station, and I was very glad to see the backs of them.

That afternoon, two women stripped to their waist, each with her hair tied in a knot behind, fought with their fists, in front of some cottages not many yards from the station platform. One woman was called 'Staffordshire Bet,' and the other 'Shropshire Sal.' They were young women, and they fought like trained prize-fighters for full ten minutes, when their hair came undone, and the men separated them. The blood streamed down each of their bodies, and either woman would have been a match for a man of moderate skill; but it was disgusting sight. The husbands seconded the women, and interference was out of the question. Blow first, and answer afterwards, would have been the reward for any disclaimer. Fight after fight occurred that night, and finally the wives changed places, and backed their husbands, who fought for double the time.

Her Most Gracious Majesty, the Queen of England, was passing my station two nights before the next Board-day, and as I had to sit up all night to see Her Majesty's train pass safely, I selected that night to search for Mr Sprigalilly's letters. It often happened, and happens still, that the station masters have to sit up all night to see Her Majesty's train through, and that although they, being salaried officers, do not receive any extra pay, as the policemen and signalmen do who are called on special duty for that work, still it has always been, and will always remain the most pleasing of all honorary duties for a station master to guard the safety of his beloved Sovereign.

I found my papers, and in the passage leading to the Board-room, on the day appointed, I found Mr Sprigalilly, who, with the exception that he had on lavender-coloured kids instead of lemon-coloured, was dressed as on the day he came to Bittern.

'Well, Mr Struggles,' said he, 'you did not send me any copies of letters you might find which had reference to this case. I suppose you could not find any.'

Had he known what I had in my paper parcel, he would not have spoken so. I did not quite like to exert the power I felt I had, and, with a view to test his better nature, I said—

'I hope, Mr Sprigalilly, you won't be too hard on me.'

'Hard on you!' said he. 'Whatever occurs you will have to thank yourself for. You come before the Directors and make a statement, and now you want to back out of that statement, and expect to get off scot free. No. I shall insist upon your proving what has been done during the last six months, and I shall demand an apology. A pretty thing, indeed!'

'Mr Sprigalilly and Mr Struggles,' said the fat man in buttons, and again I stood before the picture.

'Now, Mr Struggles,' said the Captain, 'come here.'

I went there.

'Now, then, on the last occasion you told us that you had written Mr Sprigalilly several times about no one understanding the telegraph during your absence from Bittern Station. Prove your statement.'

I opened my tissue letter copying book, and read aloud three letters addressed to Mr Sprigalilly, handing at the same time copies of them to the Directors.

'What have you to say, Mr Sprigalilly?' said the Captain.

'Mr Sprigalilly rose and said—'Gentlemen, I can assure you that I have searched my paper basket and my letter racks, and that I have no trace of any letter from Mr Struggles. Further, I am quite sure he never wrote me.'

'Very unsatisfactory,' said the Captain. 'Here are copies of three letters, duly copied in his tissue book. How do you account for it?'

Mr Sprigalilly hesitated, but at last he said—'Well, gentlemen, I don't wish to make any charge against Mr Struggles, but as regards the matter before us I am quite sure that had I received any intimation from him it would have been attended to. As I said before, I don't wish to make any accusation, but it is just possible for a letter to be written, copied, and not sent. Then, again, there may be occasional blank pages left on which a letter can be copied at a later date, but I must leave it in the hands of you to decide, gentlemen.'

This was a mean trick of Sprigalilly, and had the effect of opening my secret at once. Producing the original letter which I had written him, and which he had returned to me with a promise of attention written by himself on the back of it, I handed it in to 'The Captain.'

No man ever looked crestfallen or more contemptible than Sprigalilly when it was explained to him that his own writing belied him. For my part, I was instructed to return to my duties at once. Mr Sprigalilly endeavoured to leave the room as I did, but he was recalled to receive a Director's *blessing*. Shakespear, the booking clerk, was allowed to resume his duties, but he vowed vengeance on the Directors, and became an altered man from that date. He commenced a correspondence with Joe War, the booking clerk at Snorum, who, to my surprise, came down to spend a Sunday with him. Knowing the propensities of Joe War, I cautioned Shakespear, and I wrote to Joe to beg he would not mislead Shakespear. His answer said:—

'DEAR STRUGGLES,

'You are an old funk; and although I respect you and know you are all right, still I can't understand your writing me in such a manner— What does it mean, old man?

'Yours faithfully,

'JOE WAR.'

I knew what it meant, and Joe War knew what it meant, but I could not say more. However, I saw no more letters passing between them, and I concluded that Joe had taken the hint, and I thanked him in my heart for it.

A revolution was in store for us railway men. Our shares had depreciated in value until the matter had become serious.[1] In fact, the Great Smash Railway was all but insolvent, and only the most strenuous exertions on the part of the Directors could keep it afloat. When the most pressing matters had been attended to, the Directors turned their attention to the decrease of working expenditure. Mr McLion obtained the post of general

---

[1] In 1841–54 the Great Western Company paid an average dividend of $5\frac{1}{2}$ per cent.; in 1855–65 it was $2\frac{1}{3}$.

manager of the Great Smash Railway, and Mr McTiger, a heavy Scotchman, who had been goods' agent at Stork, succeeded Mr McLion.[1] McLion and McTiger were related by marriage, and jointly they sharpened their knives to prune down the expenditure, but jointly they first received a handsome increase of salary themselves before they commenced to hew and cut. Both of these *gentlemen* had worked up from the lowest grade of clerkship. They knew all the ins and outs of small benefices, so they know where to prune, not to make fruit, but to bleed. Now the first attacked were those whom they then thought to be the weakest, but who have since proved themselves to be the strongest, viz., the porters, police, guards, and supernumeraries. From every branch of those trees they lopped something, and 2s per week from those who had good wages. All the over-time was abolished, and about one in every fifth man was dispensed with. Next came the unfortunate clerks, and they were attacked unmercifully; £10 per annum was taken off every one of them, and a new programme was drawn up by Mr McLion for the employment of boys as clerks, instead of men, under what was termed 'Mr McLion's Lad Clerk System.' The amount to be paid to these lads was £20 per annum, instead of £50 as before, but they were promised a progressive rise of pay until they reached the magnificent sum of £50 per annum, after which time it was held out to them that even the post of general manager was open to them. The only thing my experience allows me to liken this lad clerk system, is a number of people pushing on together in an enclosed triangular passage towards the narrow point, and for whom the only escape that I can see, is to back out. Certain it is that only one can stand at the end, and that one, on the Great Smash Railway, was Mr McLion, who was all the time fattening, not only with a salary of £1,500 per annum and a percentage on the decrease of working expenses, but was allowed to sit as an arbitrator, bringing him in another £500 per annum.

The district superintendents, too, were sorted over. Those whose better feelings would not allow them to prune with merciless tyranny at the dictation of Mr McLion were reduced and placed at large stations simply as station masters, from which they had originally been promoted, and their district was added to the next man's district, which then became a division. This was an indignity which broke the heart of more than one gentlemanly superintendent.

Notices of the employment of lad clerks were posted, and it was

---

[1] John Grant, formerly Accountant for the Northern Division at Wolverhampton, succeeded Grierson as Chief Goods Manager of the Great Western Railway in 1865.

astonishing to see the number of respectable people who brought their sons to make station masters. Education, or rather the fruits of the rage for education, had just at that time commenced to show itself, and McLion was going to trade on the surplus.

Of course, the fathers and mothers looked upon the prospect of their sons ranking in public estimation and holding positions as we then did. I sincerely hope that they have not been disappointed.

Mr McTiger intimated that I must exchange at least four of my ordinary clerks, then in receipt jointly of £220, for four lad clerks at £20 each, and that must be done at once. Speedily the old clerks mentioned were removed to fill up vacancies elsewhere, and I was duly saddled with four schoolboys in place of four men. If Calcraft, the auditor, had paid me a visit he would have found fine scope for his abilities, and would have made out a report as long as my arm; but fortunately, we had a very different man as auditor, who never sponged on those whose accounts he overlooked, and who never made senseless reports.

'Are you Mr Struggles?' said a man, in plain clothes, who alighted from the train.

I explained that he was correct.

'Then,' said the stranger, 'I am a police officer in plain clothes, and I should like a few words with you in private, but not in your office, which joins the booking office, I am told. Will you meet me at the public house outside, in five minutes?'

In five minutes' time I was seated in the private parlour at the house with the police officer.

'My mission,' said he, 'is a somewhat unpleasant one, for I am instructed to take your booking clerk into custody. I have already taken War, the clerk at Snorum, and I wish to place your clerk beside him. Mr Justice and the guard Barfleet will be down by the next train with War, and we are going to take both clerks before the magistrates here, to-day. Mr Justice thought it just possible that Shakespear might get scent of what is up, and I came on to tell you to watch him.'

'What have they been doing?' I enquired.

'Well, sir,' said the detective, 'it is not for me to say, but I may tell you that, as regards that guard Barfleet, upon whose evidence they will be convicted, I rather fancy that he has done the whole thing and peached on them hoping to drag you into the mess. Have you ever quarrelled with Barfleet?'

At the moment I could not recollect having done so; but, after thinking for a while, I recollected having struck Barfleet at Puzzle Junction, for undue familiarity with myself and my tickets, and I told the detective.

'That explains all,' said he, 'but you need not take any notice; and I think, sir, you had better now go and keep your eye on Shakespear, whilst I remain here.'

On the arrival of the train by which Mr Justice and Joe War came, Shakespear, who had not the slightest suspicion of the arrival of the detective, was also handcuffed, and both clerks were taken before the bench of magistrates, who were sitting rather strongly for this case, of which they appeared to have been advised by telegraph.

The evidence against them was:—That Joe War, having assisted with the collection of tickets at Snorum, had selected twelve tickets which were issued from my station; had enclosed them in a letter to Mr Shakespear, my booking clerk, who resold them to passengers, dividing the amount realised by the second sale with Joe War. Barfleet was chief witness. He had been a paid *incognito* party to the transaction throughout, for it came out in evidence that he had always received one shilling from Joe War for delivery of the letters containing tickets to Shakespear; but whether he knew what the letters contained, and did not consider himself paid sufficiently; whether he fancied I was mixed up in the matter, or whether he exposed the fraud from motives of strict honesty due to his employers, did not transpire.

The way in which he exposed it was this. He failed to deliver one of these letters addressed to Shakespear, and he took it home instead. There he unpacked it, took the numbers of the tickets it contained, repacked and delivered them to Shakespear. Then he handed to Mr Justice the numbers of the tickets he had thus obtained, and the detective was set to work.

The tickets were resold and when they again came to hand both clerks were apprehended.

Mr Justice could not fail to accept such evidence and to act upon it, but his approval of Barfleet's conduct was pretty clearly illustrated by his saying to him in my presence, after the case was over: 'Barfleet, the case is now disposed of and the clerks have received the punishment they justly merited, but I fail to find any excuse for your having presumed to take home with you a letter or parcel which was, to all intents and purposes, the property of the Great Smash Company, and there to examine it. I have been carefully through the claims that have been paid by the Company for the value of articles which were despatched by trains of which you have been guard, and I find there are not a few cases in which the Company have paid for small articles of jewellery, &c., so intrusted. I do not pretend to make any accusation against you; but, to say the least, it is singular, and, in dismissing the matter, I now say that the very next irregularity on your part which comes before my notice will meet with very strong measures, and probably end with your dismissal. It was your duty to have taken such a parcel, if you had any suspicion as to its contents, to Mr Struggles, the station master, and not to have taken it home. Mr Struggles is quite qualified to deal with it.'

But how fared the clerks? They were both imprisoned with hard labour for six months, and, in addressing them, the chief magistrate said—

That he was 'very sorry to find two young men, well educated and with fair prospects before them, descending to such a mean offence, which not only ruined them, but which must grieve their parents.' As regards Joe War's plea that 'he was a married man with a salary of £70 per annum only' he could only say that it was a pity he had not left the service earlier, and sought a more lucrative appointment elsewhere, for which he believed he would have been qualified: but he could not accept that as any excuse for such a base fraud, and he hoped it would be a warning to others.

Joe War was a good-hearted fellow, and it was very sad to see both in such a position; but the law took its course, and printed bills announcing the conviction were posted at every station on the Great Smash Railway as a caution to others.

As War and Shakespear were getting into the train, both handcuffed, Joe War made dumb motions that he wanted to speak to me, and I went to him.

'Mr Struggles,' said Joe (he had always called me Ernest before), 'will you do me a kindness?'

I replied, 'That I would if it laid in my power.'

Poor Joe clutched my right hand with both his handcuffed ones, and said—

'I took 50 to 2 of Joe Hobbs, the bookmaker, about "Blue Gown," and and he has pulled it off. There is a writ at home, for grocery. See Joe Hobbs and hand my wife the £50, old man, or they will be turned into the street. I wouldn't care if it wasn't for them,' said Joe, and he sobbed like a child.

As for Shakespear, he showed no signs of emotion, and as the train started to take them to the county gaol I heard him telling Joe to 'be a man.'

I communicated Joe's petition to Mr Justice who said—

'Ah, poor stupid fellow! it was that betting that ruined him. He was a good clerk, and I am sorry for his family. You can go and see if you can get the £50, and hand it to his family, Mr Struggles, and I shall be able to spare you next week. I can then send some one to take charge of your station for a day or so.'

My feelings were not at all relieved by a letter I that day received from Webber, the porter at Byfield. It was a singular letter, and ran thus:—

BYFIELD STATION.

'RESPECTED SIR,

'I now write these few lines, hoping it will find you safe as it leaves me at present, but God knows, sir, things are not as they was at Byfield when you was here. That Mr Greenaway what *as* took your place is very much down on us all, and that Mr Badger what's made a divisional super. is worse nor him. Only last week Mr Greenaway reported me for not having the parcels abstracts done what you always helped me with, and Mr Badger threatened to suspend me. Sir, I have been twenty-five years here and never fined, or talked to like that before, and, sir, I wish you had never left. At times I scarce know how to put up with Mr Greenaway's nasty sayings. The more I does the less he thinks of me, and I don't think I can stand it much longer, but I thought I should like to write to you to ease my mind.

''Oping no offence,

'I am your 'umble servt.,

'J. WEBBER.'

'I never gets out with the old gun now, sir. No time for nothing.'

Poor Webber was evidently in a bad state of mind. I wrote him a nice long letter to endeavour to cheer him up, but it was returned to me by Mr Greenaway, the station master who succeeded me, together with a letter from him, as follows:—

BYFIELD STATION.

'DEAR SIR,

'The enclosed letter being addressed to Porter Webber, I opened it, as Webber has committed suicide. I have noticed him reading his Bible in the office for some days past, which he hastily put out of sight whenever I came in; and the day after he wrote you he left his work as usual, but, instead of going home, it appears he went to the river, and having tied one hand to his body, and tied his legs together in two places, he rolled himself into the water and was drowned. No one can account for his doing such a thing. The inquest on his body will take place to-night, and it is thought that it will be brought in as a case of temporary insanity.

'Yours truly,

W. GREENAWAY.

'TO MR STRUGGLES,

'Bittern.'

There was a good man lost for the sake of a friend—a kind word would have saved him! He is not the first, and he will not be the last man that sinks for the sake of a friend. Truly, this world is a world of trouble. Fortunately Webber had no family, and his wife, an excellent needlewoman, was supported by the neighbouring gentry, all of whom regretted the loss of one of the most genuine men as a railway porter who ever wore a suit of cords.

The next news from the seat of war which reached our ears, was that Mr Gabriel Gouge, the locomotive superintendent, was elected to be one of our Directors.[1] It was stated that he had possessed himself of a large number of shares in our railway, and that he was going to support Mr McLion in his endeavours to economize and recoup. A bust was erected to Mr Gouge's memory by the men who served under him as superintendent of the locomotive department; and I felt that had he taken an equal interest in the unfortunate clerks and station masters, we should not then have been handed over to Mr McLion and Mr McTiger as a body of blockheads at whose misery and expense they could derive a handsome income.

To divert my mind from the sad calamities of late, I turned my attention to the cultivation of a plot of cinder mounds adjoining and belonging to the station. I enclosed it, levelled it, hammered the cinders to pieces, and planted it with wheat. Strange to say, it grew a fair crop, and a crop of oats followed equally good. I next tried to use it as a garden, but that was a failure. The potatoes were soft, tasteless, and boiled as artichokes do, the French beans came up well, but the blacks or soot so soon accumulated on the sticks that the beans would not climb, and they did not bear. Leeks did well, and a patch of flags and a bunch of mignonette grew most luxuriantly. Acres of these cinder mounds are in this state, and it occurred to me that convicts would be well employed to reclaim the whole of them for man's use.

---

[1] Gooch became a Director in 1865.

## CHAPTER X

*Joe Hobbs—Inspector Bull meets with an Accident—I get the £50—'Relief at Lucknow'—A Runaway Engine Captured—Up before the Board—The Rev. Mr Strip in a Dilemma—Black Country Experience—A Holiday—Changes and Chances*

But how fared Joe War's wife and family? I will tell you. Mr Justice sent a substitute, and I started for Snorum.

There was Mr Peltum, with his Inspector Bull; he had been busy of late with cases for 'the Board.' Inspector Bull had been very active cutting down the men's time, and crawling about at night to catch signalmen 'on the hop,' and thus strike off their £5 annual bonus at the least possible excuse, in which he was encouraged by Mr Peltum and Mr McLion; but for which the signalmen secretly vowed vengeance against him.

I proceeded to the 'Lion' hotel to enquire as to the residence of Joe Hobbs, the bookmaker, and also that of Joe War, the booking clerk. Miss Smart was still officiating, but she had already assumed quite the landlady proportions, and of course had forgotten me.

I obtained the addresses, noting them in the pocket-book which Joe War had given me.

'Did you know Mr War?' said Miss Smart; 'he was what we call a "good-natured fool," but it won't take him long to do six months.'

Mr Hobbs, the bookmaker, was at home. At first he no doubt looked upon me as a spider looks on a fly, for he invited me into his parlour and asked me what I would take to drink.

'What is your fancy for the next race, sir?' said Mr Hobbs.

'Thank you,' I replied, 'I don't wish to back a horse. I have come on an errand from Mr War. He has commissioned me to ask you for £50, which he won on "Blue Gown," and of which his family stand in immediate need, just now.'

'He win £50 on "Blue Gown!" Me pay another man on the assertion of a man in "quod!" How would you like me to pay another man what I owed you, if you were "quodded?" Young man, you're a green 'un! you'll excuse me.'

'There is no mistake about it', said I; 'here is your writing in Mr War's pocket-book acknowledging the bet, and here is my authority to receive the money.'

'Not a bit of it, young man; I don't know your name. How do I know that the Great Smash Company won't claim this money? Besides, it's my impression it's laid off somewhere; but I am not going into any particulars with you, and not going to stir in it until Joe War comes out; and then, if it is not too hot for him about here, if he comes and squares up with me I will square up with him.'

'Sir', said I, 'as regards the Great Smash Company's claiming this money, I may tell you that I have the sanction of the superintendent to come for it and hand it to Mrs War. War was served with a writ, and without this money his furniture will be sold and his family turned into the street.'

'What have I to do with his writ, and his family, and his furniture', said Hobbs. 'Let every man mind his own business, and I should advise you to turn it up, or it may be hot for you!'

'Then, Mr Hobbs, do I understand that you refuse to pay this £50 to me for Mrs War's family?'

'Pshaw'! said Hobbs. 'do you take me for a child? How long have you left your mother?'

'Long enough to hold my own against you', I said; and, to save Mr Hobbs the trouble of ordering me off his premises, I was about to leave, when Hobbs called me back.

'Look here, young 'un', said he, 'I believe you're a bit "fly," after all. Now, take the advice of an old bird, and never stick your beak into muddy water. Here's a "fiver" for you. Take your hook, and get back to Bittern by the very next train, and don't let me hear any more of you until you want to back a horse, then Hobbs is your man; but I can't stand such outsiders as Joe War at any price.'

'Thank you', I replied; 'if I were fool enough to bet, and if this is a specimen of your payment, I should decline the honour of posting with you; and, as regards what you owe Joe War, I shall accept nothing less than the full amount. If you do not pay it I will proclaim you as a "welsher."'

'Try it on, young man', said Joe Hobbs, 'and if you interfere with me I will give you something for your trouble.'

Now this was anything but pleasant business, and I was at a loss to know how to act; but I determined to get the money, if possible. It was no good my going to see Mrs War without the £50, so I strolled down to the station.

Some porters and policemen were talking in a group on the platform, and all seemed in high glee.

'Serve him right!' said one.

'Great pity he didn't kill him!' said another.

'How did it happen?' said a third.

The porter questioned thus related it:—

'Why, old Inspector Bull has been going prowling about for weeks past, at night. He caught one man nodding in his box, and reported him asleep; and he caught another not putting his signal on before the train was fairly past it, and reported him; and he caught another one with a pot of beer in a can, and all these men lost their bonuses. Last night, he went down by the "goods" to Hinehoe station, and started to walk back at midnight to catch them all. You know "Whiskery Bill," that chap as went away from here 'cos Bull caught him smoking at one o'clock in the morning, and was took off two shillings a week and moved. Well, "Whiskery Bill" was on the look-out for Bull, and as old Bull came creeping along "Whiskery Bill" rushes out of his box and knocks him down with a crowbar, and stuns Bull. He aint come properly round yet. Aint it a lark!'

'Lark'! said another, 'but what will they do to "Whiskery Bill?"'

'Why they can't do nothing. He has got a very good excuse. Someone cut one of the telegraph wires there last week, and he says he thought Bull was a burglar or wire-cutter, and struck him before he found it out.'

The train arrived, and with it came Inspector Bull, on a hurdle, in the luggage van. There was some difficulty in obtaining four volunteers to carry Mr Peltum's bully to his home, until Mr Peltum himself named four for the office. No sooner had the procession left the station than all the other men assembled in the refreshment room and drank to the health of 'Whiskery Bill,' and to the non-recovery of Inspector Bull.

Inspector Bull did recover, but he never prowled about at night afterwards.

Not forgetting the usual hour for assembly at the 'Lion,' for those who wished to back horses, and play at billiards, I made my way thither. I was a stranger to those assembled, among whom were several of the students from the College. They were fine young men, probably training for the Church, but they liked to back a horse for all that, and Joe Hobbs was registering their bets somewhat freely

Addressing the whole body from a chair, I said:—

'Gentlemen,—I have come to Snorum on a very unpleasant mission. Will you allow me to say a few words?'

'Down with him!' said Joe Hobbs.

'Out with him!' said Joe Hobbs's tout.

'Fair play', said the students; 'give him a hearing.'

As the students predominated, and as Joe Hobbs did not wish to offend them, order was at last restored. I continued—

'I once had a friend. That friend has a wife and two little children, but he has got into trouble and has gone to prison for six months. Before he got into trouble he took a bet of £50 to 2 against "Blue Gown," the horse that won. He asked me to see the party with whom he bet, and to get the £50 to save his furniture being sold and his wife and little children turned out in the street. That man refused to pay——'

'Who is he? Who is he?' said a dozen voices.

Joe Hobbs sidled round to me, and I felt the crisp, welcome feel of bank notes, which he was trying to push into my hand. I allowed him to place them there, and, closing my hand, I said—

'Gentlemen,—I will call on the party once more, and if he does not pay I will come and give you his name.'

'Do', said they, 'and we will give him such a ducking this night as he never received before.'

I slipped out, and counted the notes. The amount was there, save the £2 posted, and with £50 for Mrs War I very soon presented myself at her cottage. In answer to my knock, she looked out of the upstairs window and enquired who I was. I produced Joe War's pocket-book, and she very soon opened the door. As I sat down on a chair, she sank on to the sofa and, exclaiming 'Thank God'! she fainted. There was a dear little trot, a little girl about four years of age, the image of Joe War; even her tiny mouth was cut a little on one side, so closely did she resemble her father.

'I taught it was my pappa', said the little thing. 'When's my pappa tomin' home? Naughty man, my pappa, stay away so long.'

Mrs War had no servant, so I was obliged to search for cold water and towel, and to make use of my experience as to the application of necessary restoratives. The baby awoke in its cradle, and, together with its cries and the application of cold water, Mrs War 'came round', as the old nurses call it. A rat-tat-tat at the front door finally aroused her.

'Don't open the door', said Mrs War, 'I expect it is the bailiffs come to take all our things. Mr Struggles, What shall I do?'

'Keep them out, Mrs War', said I, 'and I will see what can be done; but once let them in, and you are at their mercy. See to your windows and fastenings—'

'Oh! the upstairs window', said Mrs War, and she flew to it.

Already the bailiff was half in: another moment it would have been too late, but down went the window, and Mrs War jammed his knuckles between the window and the sill. The man swore, but withdrew his hands, and the window was closed and fastened.

There were two of them, and the elder one enquired of Mrs War as to whether she knew who he was. Said he—

'I am the Sheriff's officer for the county, and I have a warrant in my pocket for your goods. If you refuse to admit me, I will get a police officer and break open the door. Stupid woman, you are doing no good. If you still resist me, I will bring a broker and sell everything you have, in the street, now; but if you let me in peaceably I may show you some leniency.'

'What am I to do, Mr Struggles'? said the poor, frightened woman.

'I wish my pappa was here; he would kill him', said the poor little child.

I advised Mrs War not to let them in, but to let me out and I would parley with them, assuring her that I would not desert her, but strictly counselling her not to admit them.

At first, the Sheriff's officer ignored my interference, but when I handed him a £5 note to secure his own expenses, and requested him to accompany me to the claimant, he became an altered man. I took care first to take the Sheriff's officer to an hotel, and to stroke down his ruffled feathers. Next we proceeded to the grocer at whose instance the seizure was made, and finally I settled the whole thing for £20, and the bailiff who had been parading round the house was withdrawn.

Mrs War fell on her knees and kissed my hand. It was quite a young 'relief at Lucknow.' I handed her £30 to keep her going, and by letting lodgings and selling a few articles she managed to rub along until Joe came out, when they emigrated to America.

My old engine-driver, Mad Sandy, was still on the shunting engine to which he had been reduced at Fame, and as I was waiting to be conveyed back to Bittern he called from his engine to me, as follows:—

'Beg your pardon, Mr Struggles, but your train won't be down for ten minutes. I hope no offence, sir; I can't leave my engine, but I *should* very much like to speak to you.'

With this invitation, I jumped off the platform, and, crossing the line to the siding where Mad Sandy's engine was standing in readiness to do any shunting that might be required of him, I mounted his foot-plate.

'Well, sir', said Sandy, wiping his hands with some cotton waste, 'and how are you, and how is the missis, and how many do you muster in family now, sir?'

I told him that Mrs Struggles had added a little daughter to our establishment, when he laughed aloud, and said—

'Bless me, sir, why that's only two now. Why, my old doommon[1] has just got twins, and that's thirteen, Mr Struggles, and only one of 'em that earns a sixpence. What I want to ask you, sir, is if you can't get me put on as a goods' driver again. I've been here ever since I frightened that old man to death at the crossing, and I don't think he would have lived till now, Mr Struggles, if I hadn't frightened him. I wish you would just write a letter for me, Mr Struggles. It's no good speaking to that old Mr Peltum, for if he once rounds on a man its all up with him.'

A sudden consternation was visible amongst the *employés* at the station. Mr Peltum was not there, but the telegraph boy came rushing from his office, and it was soon explained that a telegraphic message had been received to the effect that an engine in full steam had, by some extraordinary means, escaped from Borum station, without driver or stoker upon her, and was on her way to Snorum station.

'Open all the points and let her run through', said the Inspector; 'its no good trying to stop her. The only chance is that she may run herself down before she gets to London.'

Mad Sandy grasped my arm—

'Mr Struggles', said he, 'when she runs through, don't say anything, but just open those points and let me out after her. I'll stop her—just see if I don't. Jump up again, and come along with us. *Do, sir!*'

The runaway engine was then sighted, and but for man's invention of the telegraph having overtaken the invention of the steam-engine, a dreadful calamity might have happened; as it was, everyone gasped for breath as the engine rattled through the station. I had barely time to turn the points and to jump on Mad Sandy's engine before he was on her track, but the 'Empress'[2] —for that was the name of the runaway engine—had a tremendous start of us. Grave as was the moment, and terrific the pace at which we were soon travelling, Sandy was in ecstasies. He danced on the foot-plate, and sang the first verse of his favourite song, '*A rummy old cadger am I. Ha! ha!*'

'We're gaining on her', he exclaimed, 'we shall have her before she gets to Puzzle Junction, Mr Struggles; but hasn't she got some steam? I wonder how she got away.'

The telegraph had cleared the way, and as we rattled on under the bridges and past the small stations we could hear the lusty old English cheer,

---

[1] Woman.

[2] No engine of this name appears in the list of broad-gauge locomotives given in MacDermot's *History*.

'Hurrah! hurrah!' as it became evident to the on-lookers that we were overtaking the 'Empress.'

Our engine fairly jumped as she gained on her. Mad Sandy stirred his fire furiously, put on more steam, and buttoned his coat. By this time we were within sight of Puzzle Junction, and for nine miles we had raced the 'Empress', but it seemed only a few moments, the excitement was intense.

'Now, mate,' said Sandy, 'I'm going to jump, and if I miss—God help the little ones!'

His lip quivered, his eyes filled with water, and grasping my hand and saying 'You won't forget 'em, Mr Struggles', he crawled along to the front of his engine, which was by this time close behind the tender of the runaway 'Empress,' to jump on to her.

There stood the father of thirteen children on the buffer-beam of his engine, ready to make the awful leap. Perhaps, some would have tried to jump on to the coals, but Sandy knew better, and with a cat-like spring he grasped the end of the tender attached to the 'Empress', and, turning round, he held out one arm to us to signify 'all right.' Another minute, and he had climbed round to the engine, shut off steam, and was in the act of performing some most extraordinary antics on the foot-plate as we neared Wilderness Road Station.

Mad Sandy met with much well-deserved praise for this splendid stroke of business. The Directors presented him with £5 for his bravery, and he is again a regular engine-driver on the Great Smash Railway.

The engine had been put in motion by a schoolboy, who, during the temporary absence of the driver and his mate, had stepped on to the engine and turned on the steam. He was so frightened at what he had unconsciously done, that he jumped off immediately and left her to proceed as described.

The lad clerks at Bittern very soon sickened of their occupation. Their parents began to find it expensive to maintain and to clothe them, and the lads being, by nature of their occupation, brought into connection with men of business, doubtless found it inconvenient to be without pocket money.

No less than four cases of petty larceny occurred among my poor clerks in less than six months. One stole the postage stamps, and, indeed, this kind of pilfering was so general that stamps were shortly afterwards perforated with the Company's initials. Another collected an account for railway carriage, and failed to account for it; a third sold a ticket, and omitted to book it up; and the fourth stole half a sovereign from the till. Although Mr McLion clamoured loudly for the public punishment of each in his turn, I managed in the case of all, save the half-sovereign, to restrain the anger of the Directors, and to allow the parents to make it up; but Mr McLion would not abate his anger in the case of the half-sovereign, and, as a warrant was issued for the apprehension of the offender, he escaped to some other land, but was afraid to advise his sorrowing mother, who was a widow, of his whereabouts. Many were the tears this poor woman shed in my house and my office.

With these troublesome youngsters, who rarely did any work during my absence, I found it very difficult to spare the time to collect the ledger accounts and to canvass for traffic. Was it, therefore, to be wondered at that I expended £15 on a cob pony, to assist me in this duty? There was always sufficient corn, chaff, &c., swept out of the mangers of the cart horses to keep a rough pony, and I was just congratulating myself on the time I thus saved when an order to attend before the Board of Directors in London, on the following Board day, on a charge of keeping a horse on the Company's provender, was forwarded to me by Mr McTiger.

Only those who have held similar appointments can understand the distaste that a railway man has for going before his Board of Directors on a charge of this kind. Although the charge may be petty, and the man may struggle through it without any positive blame, still it weighs heavily on a man of sensitive feeling from the time he receives the order until he presents himself before the Board. Everything a railway man has of value he takes with him on the day he has to appear before his Directors. His character, his long service, his hopes, and the older he becomes the more he has at stake.

'Well, my dear, how did you get on?' says his wife, the moment he returns, for she, too, dreads the uncertainty of the decision of the Directors.

Besides which, there is an awful amount of annoyance connected with an order to attend before the Board. The order is copied by the clerks in the Superintendent's office. It becomes small talk immediately, and although it burns in one's pocket you are continually twitted by your fellow clerks or station masters, by gentle reminders—such as, 'Hulloa, old fellow! going to see the Picture on Board Day?' And even on your journey to London, the fellows 'twig' you and pop their head in, as the train is starting from each station, just to say, 'Give my love to the Captain'; or, 'Glad its you instead of me, going to see the Picture.'

The night before I went up I had a dream. I always dreamt before I went before the Board.

I thought I was in front of a racing stand, in which was seated the Captain as judge. Messrs. McLion and McTiger were mounted on elephants, Mr Justice on a black charger, Mr Calcraft on a unicorn, and Mr Badger on a donkey. It was to be a race for my liberty, but why or wherefore I could not understand. At a given signal we all started, and the donkey led. I knew I could pass him, and did not hurry. Calcraft was behind on the unicorn; Mr Justice on his black charger rode by my side, and my cob went merrily. At last the momentous time arrived as we were nearing the winning post, and I put spurs to my cob to pass the donkey, but the elephants closed me in and I could not escape to pass, although my animal could have done it easily. The Captain was waving his flag, and, as a last hope, I tried to pull up to escape from the pressure of the elephants, who had wound their trunks in front of me; but, alas! Calcraft on his unicorn was behind, and the animal thrust his horn into my cob, which sprang forward, and I was crushed between the elephants.

'My dear', said my wife, 'are you not going up with the Cash train, this morning? It is only half-an-hour to the time.'

This was reality—the other was a dream—and again at 11 A.M. I stood before the 'Picture.'

This time with tolerable success, for, having provided myself with letters from the chief traders and shareholders in the neighbourhood of my station, to the effect that they never saw the company's horses looking so well, and that the business of the company was never so well attended to.

The Captain actually said that the Directors were pleased to have so good an account of me, but that they could not sanction my keeping a horse on the company's corn, or other station masters would do the same, and probably use it for their own amusement.

Mr McTiger was not complimented as to his zeal on this occasion, but he sharpened his knife against me on our return.

One, Mr Cromo, a prosperous merchant and a large shareholder in the Great Smash Company, had given me a strong letter of recommendation; and, wishing to thank him and advise him of my success, I took an early opportunity of calling upon him.

'Come in, Mr Struggles come in. How did you get on? Of course, I knew the Directors wouldn't say anything to you. What a strange thing it is that they can't manage their affairs without employing those hard-headed Scotchmen to destroy every bit of good feeling that exists between themselves and the public, and the men and their employers. If you are not particularly engaged, I wish you would stay half-an-hour. I want to ask your opinion as to the position of your company.'

'I am afraid', I replied, 'that my opinion is not of much value, but you are indeed welcome to it.'

'It is just this, Struggles. I have a good many shares in your line, and

I see that they are down in the market as low as £40. I am pressed to take up more at that price. What do you think of it?'

'I think, sir, you cannot possibly go wrong. They cannot go lower.'

'Why not?' enquired Mr Cromo. 'What do you think of McLion's policy of decreasing the working expenses?'

'Upon my word, Mr Cromo, I scarcely like to express my ideas on such a subject, it is the day-dream of all us subordinates.'

'Nonsense', said he, 'you can trust me. I should not ask your opinion if I did not value it. You are a practical railway officer.'

'Well, sir, then my opinion is this—Railways are the high roads of the country. Every day adds to the houses and to the population in the immediate vicinity of the stations, and necessarily the traffic increases. I see no reason why all railways should not, one day, pay ten per cent.; but the steps the Directors are now taking are as ill-judged as the opposition to the making of railways was in its day.'

'You refer to the cutting down process, I presume', remarked Mr Cromo.

'I do, sir; and although it may have a temporary tendency to produce a dividend it is bound to end in disaster. There is not a man in the service of a railway company but who has it in his power to add to, or diminish, the shareholders' dividend. If a station master is worried and ill-paid, will he canvass for traffic, economize as regards labour, or consumption of stores, gas, &c.? If the drivers and guards are discontented, will they exert themselves to keep time and save the running of special trains necessitated by their being late? If the porters are angry, will they pack and unpack damageable articles carefully, to avoid claims for damage? Take the case of a goods' guard, who, on taking his fortnight's wage, finds that three shillings have been struck off his overtime; follow that guard with his train to the next station, where he unhooks his engine and goes into a siding for three trucks containing cast iron grates, crates of glass, and cases of eggs. He is cross, and he calls out to his driver, "Hit 'em up, Bill"; and Bill does hit them up with three times the required force, and when the three trucks come in contact with the train, they actually rebound. Then follow those goods to their stations of destination, and I will wager that twenty pounds does not pay the damage the goods have sustained. Now, what is the value of the three shillings saved by Mr McLion? And so on throughout. In fact, the companies are at variance with the only sure means of their prosperity—and that is the co-operation of the *employés*. It is useless to deal with these skilled labourers as if they were navvies loading clay by the yard; and half the time now bestowed on the grinding down of these men would produce a system by which every railway man could be an interested shareholder in the railway he labours on, by providing for that man a provision for old age. Then you would have interested labour, although even then it would still cost every railway company £50—in damage and neglect—for the training of a simple porter.'

'Well done, Struggles!' exclaimed Mr Cromo, 'there is a great deal of truth in what you say, but I am afraid it will be a long time before you convince the Directors that an experienced railway man is of any value—particularly in the clerk department. This country will be all clerks presently. I asked Mr Justice the other day how much money he allows these new twenty-pounds-a-year-clerks to handle, and he tells me that they are all insured for £300 in some guarantee office.'

'I pity the shareholders in that guarantee company.'

'Aye, Struggles! Well, I shall take up some more shares, and risk it.'

Mr Cromo did take up some more shares, and they doubled in value in a very short space of time.

Adjoining the station was the clergyman's house. The Rev. Strip[1] was quite an aristocrat, but I think he must have been very unhappy, as there were no people in Bittern with manners or habits in accordance with his taste, and he walked abroad unheeded and alone. His church, too, was nearly empty, and the only flourishing thing in his dominion was the horseradish in the churchyard. This was very fine indeed, and when the gravedigger opened the ground, report said he made a good thing of the horseradish.

The Rev. Strip had a door communicating with the passenger platform, and he often came out to look at the trains, and we occasionally consoled each other by talking about the beauties of other places.

'I tried very hard', said he, 'to make some impression on these people when I came, and one of the first things I did was to hold a confirmation. Amongst the candidates for confirmation was a woman quite forty years of age, and when questioned as to the number of commandments, she replied that there were three only. I requested her to name them. She said they were "Easter, Whitsuntide, and Bittern Wake!" So you see what a dreadful state of ignorance I have to contend with; indeed, it seems ridiculous to send missionaries abroad with such a state of things at home.'

This gentleman appeared one evening, and, inviting me into his study, unburdened himself in the following manner:—

'Mr Struggles,—Something tells me that I can trust you, and I am going to tell you of a most diabolical outrage that was committed on me to-day,

[1] The Rev. A. Shepp.

in your trains. I was travelling to Stork in a first-class carriage, and at the station between this one and Stork, a well-dressed woman got into my compartment. The train had barely started when she came and sat most deliberately in front of me, and demanded a sovereign. I need not tell you that we were alone, and that when I had sufficiently recovered from the shock which her outrageous conduct necessarily occasioned, I informed her of my intention of giving her into custody at the next station. This had no effect whatever upon her; and, unbinding her hair and disarranging her attire, to show the semblance of a scuffle, she coolly replied—

'Very well; you know your own business best. It may, or may not, answer your purpose. You may, or may not, be believed. Is a sovereign of so much value to you that you prefer to risk your reputation to assisting one who is in great need of it?'

'When she had done speaking I fairly trembled, and, unmanned for the moment, I gave her the sovereign. She readjusted her hair and dress, and disappeared in an instant when the train arrived at Stork.'

'Mr Struggles, you laugh', said the Rev. Strip; 'what makes you do so?'

'I was thinking, sir, what a very narrow escape you had, how wise you were to pay the sovereign. If a gentleman like yourself is accused of doing wrong, there are always some uncharitable people ready to believe he is guilty. But can't we catch this veritable lady? What sort of a person was she?'

'Precisely so', said the rev. gentleman. 'I am, indeed, glad I told you about it; but, on your honour, if I hand you this written description of the woman, you will promise not in any way to mention my name in connection with the matter, unless a similar charge can be preferred by another party, in which case I would readily come forward. Will you offer a reward of one pound to anyone who will assist you to trace the woman?'

It was no easy matter to act the detective in this quiet manner, but at last I determined to offer the reward to one of the guards who was constantly in charge of trains up and down this line. He was not a man I liked, for he was an impudent guard, and often appeared from the wrong part of his train when it stopped, neglecting his brake; indeed, it was said of him, that he knew everybody's business, and walked up and down the train outside, as it was in motion, looking into the windows to see what was going on. In the darkness of the night, and with lights inside the compartment, a man so watching is not visible. At the same time, I thought he would be the right man to employ, and I told him of the case and offered him the one pound reward, should he succeed in bringing the guilty party to light.

He readily undertook the task; and said that he thought he knew the woman, and would—to use his words—'watch her little games.'

A week later, this guard was found with his head smashed, by reason of its coming into contact with a bridge, possibly, whilst he was leaning forward to look into the next carriage, and with his death our search for the woman ended.

Although my representation of Bittern is not likely to impress my readers favourably as to the people living there, it is only fair that I should speak of them as I found them.

It was no uncommon thing for murders and drunken brawls to occur in the neighbourhood, and many acts of cruelty were related. I ascended to the top of the blast furnace where a man threw his donkey in, and actually burnt it, because he was offended with it. I descended into the coal-pit where a man was thrown and lived for a week on snails and frogs; and more than once I saw hair and blood sticking to the brickwork of the railway arch hard by, the result of some foul play.

On one occasion, two boys scarcely fourteen years of age, backed by a number of colliers, were fighting just outside the station, and, disgusted with the language and directions that were hurled at these youths—both of whom were completely spent with a long fight,—I caught hold of them, and dragging them into the station closed the doors on the mob. Having put an end to their quarrel, I enquired the reason of their fighting and this was the boy's answer:—

'That boy and me works together in a colliery. He has been bad this week, and hasn't been to work. I've earnt thirty shillings this week and I've gave him half, and now he wants to fight me!'

Both boys looked as pale as death, and although they earned such good wages probably their life would be a short one. Perhaps, they would become puddlers when they were twenty years of age, and work red-hot iron, when they would earn four and five pounds per week, and then they would become old men at the age of thirty-five, and possibly die devoid of common necessaries.

Despite their roughness, I never received an insult from a collier or iron-worker. I traversed the district for six miles round, often on foot and late in the evening, and sometimes with hundreds of pounds in my pocket collected for the company, but I often received an invitation to drink with them; or, perhaps, they craved permission to come and look at my black pig, with ten little black pigs, for strange as the anomaly may seem with such surroundings, black pigs were a novelty in that neighbourhood.

Sunday morning was their great time for exercising fighting-cocks, bulldogs, and short clay pipes. After a very pressing invitation, I once went to a low public house hard by to see 'Jim Slogger's dogs.' Jim Slogger was a fighting man, and he had the best dogs in the neighbourhood. They all lived indoors, and he exercised them in a large loft upstairs. Although I was always fond of dogs, I was delighted to get out of his house, for the dogs were so large and so savage. They fought each other, irrespective of sex or parentage, as directed; and he got them into condition by instructing them to worry a roller for hours together, in the loft before described. I should have preferred to face a wolf to either of them, but my friend encouraged me by saying—

'Yow needna be afraid. He wunna worry yow wi'out oi tells him.'

Mr Bead, whose son was the Mayor, had a bull mastiff, the admiration of everyone in that neighbourhood. No matter the weather, he exercised his dog every evening himself, and more than once he took me to see it chained to an iron kennel with an iron paving for a yard. He went into his meadows as usual to air the dog, one evening, but he did not return, and his daughter became anxious about him; at last, a search was instituted, and Mr Bead was found insensible, and savaged in the most dreadful manner by his own dog, which crept home to its kennel when discovered. The poor old gentleman, quite sixty years of age, was taken home; and when his son arrived and heard of the occurrence, his first act was to seize an iron bar and attack and kill the dog that had so mangled his father.

For many weeks Mr Bead's life was despaired of, but gradually he recovered and with his own lips he related the occurrence to me, as follows:—

'I was just stooping under the rail of the fencing which divides my meadows when, I suppose, my dog mistook me for someone else. At any rate, he seized me and commenced to worry me. I called him by name, even patted him whilst he bit me, did everything, but it was no good; and when I hit him he was more savage still. I managed, however, to keep him from my throat, and he commenced biting both legs, from my thighs downwards. In fact, the doctor said my legs could not have been worse if I had a charge of shot in both of them. At last, being very fat, he grew tired and laid down beside me. Although I was faint from the loss of blood and my strength almost gone, I began to see some hope, and I managed to get my pen-knife out of my pocket, but I had no strength left to open it; still the dog laid there. Presently I caught the point of the knife in my clothes, and this opened it. Then I rolled over with the pen-knife open and stuck it into the dog. He was too much exhausted to move, and when I saw the blood come I continued to stick the knife into him. At last he got up and crawled away from me, but I had no strength to move and I laid there until my dear daughter found me.'

What with a new booking-clerk, the lad clerks in the Goods' station, and Mr McTiger's daily irony, I began to feel very unwell, and applied for a few days' leave of absence.

'You had better take it at once', said Mr Justice, 'as great changes are likely to take place, and I fear that there will be no leave of absence granted for some time when they commence.'

I took him at his word, and, packing up the old gun, some fishing tackle, &c., I paid a long promised visit, together with young 'Dido', to an old schoolmate—a farmer—and to my relations.

To wake up and find you are free of trains, managers, and accounts, is in itself a sufficient romance for the first day of a railway man's holiday, and to be able to unstring one's self and lie down in an orchard under a tree, *out of sound of a railway whistle*, is a perfect elysium, to say nothing of a quiet chat with nice old friends, who actually don't want a railway ticket, a claim settled, or haven't positively a railway grievance. In the evening you can get fishing rods ready and your baits for the next day's fishing, and sit on the lawn and see the dear old sun set, and go to bed another man. Then, with a nice little luncheon, you can take yourself off to the river, and, selecting a quiet spot, prepare for a fish.

Companions I needed none, as I fished quietly in that back stream in a sheltered corner, on the second morning of my holiday. I was only too delighted to be alone.

Opposite me was an osier bed, an island in itself, of which, by the holes, it would appear that the water rats were the population. The dragon-fly skimmed the water in front of me, the swallows dashed in pursuit of the gnats, and that everlasting little chattermag, the white-throat, was busy making its nest in the rushes. I was patiently waiting for a bite, without moving a muscle, when, glancing across to the island, I noticed that I was not alone, for the water rats were sitting outside their holes, gnawing the rushes. Their sharp teeth made quick work of them, and every now and then they washed their funny little faces, and looked the picture of happiness. Nature supplied each family with a mud house, and food grew just outside the front door. No directors, no general manager, no Calcraft, for them! and I was mentally comparing their happy life with my own, when plump went No. 1 water rat; another second, and plump went No. 2; No. 3, ditto, and so on all round, as far as I could see or hear them. This was very strange conduct; perhaps it was bathing time, or, maybe, they felt too warm. A bite from a good strong perch then attracted my attention, and, having landed it, I again composed myself. The rats did the same, and went on gnawing the rushes, until a terrific scramble convinced me that something was amiss with them; and, looking up, I saw one, a fine fat fellow, plump into the water only just in time to save himself from the fangs of a hungry stoat closely in pursuit. The rat dived, but the stoat went on round the island in pursuit of others, and as he proceeded I could hear rats plump into the water to save their lives.

No doubt this wretched stoat kept going round his district until he caught some poor rat in low water, and dragged him up for 'board'; and his operations were so analogous to those of Calcraft on the railway, that I pitied those poor rats; so much so, that I returned to the farmhouse for my gun, and, waiting for an opportunity, I shot the stoat to save the rats further trouble, leaving it there for the rats to hold a 'wake' over its body.

My string of roach and perch made a nice fry for supper, and the next day my friend arranged to go shooting with me.

What a splendid day we had of it. How his old retriever followed a hare, which my friend had wounded, by scent full two miles in sight of us on the hill, true to an inch, and then brought her back to us. How we laughed as we saw the old dog try to jump the wire fencing with her, and eventually, putting the hare down, jump it himself, and drag the hare through at the bottom and bring her on; and how my friend praised me for an excellent shot at a pheasant, skimming the tops of the trees over our heads.

'How did you manage to kill that bird' ? he asked.

'Why, if you must know, I shot underneath, and I believe I allowed quite a foot when I pulled, for she was going express.'

What a jolly evening we spent. How we sang all the old songs we could think of, and finally sent old Farmer Stilton home on his old mare, with his saddle turned the wrong way and the reins tied to her tail. 'Steady, mare,' said the farmer, as she evinced some slight disposition to kick when her master pulled the reins; but she walked quietly off with him, and, more asleep than awake, Mr Stilton arrived safely at his farm, much to the amusement of his man, who was sitting up for him.

But these are all matters of the past. Nevertheless, they all tended to put new life into me for my occupation, and I returned to Bittern quite another man.

The worst part of a railway man's holiday is that when he returns he finds such heaps of work in arrear. There are so many matters that cannot progress during his absence, for railway correspondence is, as a rule, a tissue of inventions, so that if anyone but the inventor goes on with it the whole thing becomes entangled.

If a claim, for instance, is reported, the manager commences to try and pick a hole in the coat of someone connected with the staff of the station which reports it, instead of dealing with the case in a business-like manner; and if a station master is not almost a lawyer, he will suddenly find himself bowled out and ordered up before the Board on a charge of which he was at the onset entirely innocent. To save this, he has to defend himself against managers and inspectors with all sorts of cunning and improper fabrications known only to railway men, which, if not amounting to lies, are very strong prevarications.

As a case in point, I have known a claim paid for an article supposed to have been sent by train and never received; and although the checker swore it was loaded, the goods' guard swore he put it out at its destination, and the receiving station master swore he received it and handed it to the agent for delivery, it is, perhaps, found behind a lot of sacks in the goods station, from which it was never despatched. Such an article would be pushed into some passing truck, and, arriving in London or elsewhere, unentered and unclaimed, would be sold in the annual sale as unowned; and simply because the man who found it was afraid to speak the truth.

Directors and managers think a great deal of their system of correspondence and enquiry, but I am wicked enough not to value it to the extent of the paper it is written on, so far as it is supposed to contain the facts of any case before them.

By the time that I had waded through these matters in arrear, and made the monthly collection of accounts, Mr Justice appeared with important news.

'Mr Struggles', said he, 'Mr McLion has decided to divide the passenger and goods' departments in this district. Would you like to take the goods' department at the same salary and give up the house, with the prospect of a £10 rise in place of it, if Mr McTiger recommends it in a few months' time?'

I thanked Mr Justice, and positively declined the honour of—at the very least—a £30 fall for the prospect of a most uncertain £10 rise.

Mr McTiger, too, tried his persuasive powers, by saying—

'Struggles, now you know I have had a great deal of trouble with you, and now that you have just got into my ways you are going to leave me, and, possibly, against your own interest.'

I thanked him, also, most politely, but positively declined the honour.

'We shall not make the change for a week', said Mr Justice, 'but until we find you another station, I shall be glad of your assistance in my office; as my assistant superintendent, Mr Bowler, has inherited some property and left the service.'

'*Happy man!*'

Accordingly, an inspector at £20 per annum less than I was taking, was sent to take charge of Bittern station, and I repaired to assist Mr Justice at Bass station.

But I may as well tell you that a committee was formed by the ironmasters and inhabitants, who invited me to a supper party and presented me with a handsome gold watch, on which is engraved—

'Presented to Mr Ernest Struggles by the ironmasters and inhabitants of Bittern, as a token of their esteem for the attentive manner in which he discharged his duties as agent for the Great Smash Railway.'

A pleasing token of remembrance of which I shall ever be proud.

In my new temporary engagement I was clerk to the divisional superintendent. He rode round his district with £500 per annum and expenses for refreshments; whilst I sat in his office all day and kept his clerks in order, prepared returns of traffic, compared expenses of wages for three years, and re-echoed the thunder from Messrs. McLion, McTiger, and Fretsum, on the heads of the unhappy clerks and station masters. This, then, was the chief post of promotion which I, as a station master, could aspire to, viz., the post of Divisional Superintendent, at a salary varying according to circumstances, from £250 to £500 per annum. Hitherto that post had been a most gentlemanly occupation, and the person holding the appointment had enjoyed the exercise of discriminating power in many matters that worked most beneficially for the interest of the Company and the social position of himself and family: but under the new system these men were denuded of all but petty power, and became merely communicators of Mr McLion's thunder and lightning. All feeling was out of the question, and any human edifice that remained for long without a lightning conductor was speedily struck by the flash, and removed as a useless structure to make room for the great element.

One gentleman who ascended the platform of reform even ventured to boast that he ran about without shoes in his infancy, and lived upon porridge. He did not hesitate to compare his early expenses with those of any applicant for an advance of pay, and we all abandoned hope of advancement or redress; and when I now see a gentleman, a railway superintendent, practising charity in the village where he resides, I am inclined to ask myself—'Is that man dissembling, or does he practice philanthropy at his office?'

There was no mistake about the energy of Mr McLion, and the purport of his letters to Mr Justice were to the effect that unless the expenses were immediately decreased his own position was at stake, and Mr Justice conformed to his directions.

Mr O'Reilly, on the other hand, very soon disagreed with Mr McLion; and, an exchange between himself and Mr Justice being arranged, the latter gentleman went to London, where he was further promoted to be superintendent of the line.[1]

In point of practical railway management, Mr O'Reilly was, in my humble opinion, far superior to Mr McLion, but he had omitted to apply his attention to the value of goods' traffic, and he had not the patience to accept dictatorial directions from inexperienced gentlemen amongst the directory; so down came Mr O'Reilly from the summit eminence of traffic superintendent of the whole line, to the direction of a part only of the system. Although his manner was austere and his directions peremptory, Mr O'Reilly was a most fair dealing man, who would always take the part of a good man against an unjust attempt to oust him.

Railway service would be a very different occupation had such men as my old friend in the 'picture' and Mr O'Reilly remained at the helm.

'Struggles', said Mr O'Reilly, 'I have a letter from Mr Justice. He offers you —— station. You ought, I am sure, to think yourself highly honoured. I always picked the smartest man I could find for that station. Of course, you will accept it, but I shan't let you go until McLion sends a man to take your place.'

That night I had a most extraordinary dream again.

I was at one time in custody of several lunatics. At another I was thrashing Mr Badger with an ash stick. Then I was receiving presents from royal personages. Again, I was smoking a pipe with Mr John Brown; and then, again, came the race against the donkey, with the elephants crushing me. All, doubtless, the effect of having eaten a crab for supper. But stay—

'Was it all, or any part of it, to come true?'

Read PART THE SECOND, when it is published, and you will see.

---

[1] Tyrrell became Superintendent of the Line on 1 February 1864.